PASTOR [

SOAK

EXPERIENCING THE TRANSFORMING POWER OF GOD'S PRESENCE

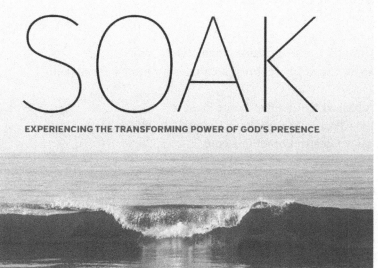

Creative Force Press

Creative Force Press

SOAK
© 2015 by Dave Minton
www.go2ccc.org

This title is also available as an eBook. Visit
www.CreativeForcePress.com/titles for more information.

Published by Creative Force Press
4704 Pacific Ave, Suite C, Lacey, WA 98503
www.CreativeForcePress.com

ISBN: 978-1-939989-22-2

Printed in the United States of America

DEDICATION

I would like to dedicate this book to the Capital Christian Center family who constantly amaze me with their desire to deepen their relationship with God.

It's an honor to serve you.

TABLE OF CONTENTS

Introduction

Have you ever been on a great journey? This idea of *"SOAK"* is about going on a journey. It's about going on a trip to a new place.

My wife, Kelly, and I had the opportunity to travel to Europe. What an amazing journey it was. We took pictures, we met people and we saw things. We could sit down and talk to you for hours about the things we learned, the things we saw and the many things we experienced. It was great! Some of the buildings we visited took hundreds of years to build. I pondered that, and thought *wow, I'm trying to build a church in my lifetime and some of these communities worked on one building for hundreds of years.* They were incredible, historical monuments.

When you go on a good journey, on a good adventure, you have good memories. Your good experiences will stay with you for a lifetime. And, when you go on a spiritual journey, there are amazing things you will experience that will also stay with you for a lifetime and beyond.

Not only do we have the opportunity to go on physical journeys, we can also go on emotional journeys. Maybe you meet someone new, and you start to get excited about that relationship. Courtship begins, then you move towards engagement and you get married. Remember the emotional journey of dating and getting married and how fun and exciting that was? A lot of people say, "I wish I could go back and get that feeling." It is so emotionally powerful.

When women become pregnant and feel a child growing on the inside of them, they think *this is incredible. How could a living being be on the inside of me?* They eventually give birth to those children, and everyone around them got to watch the whole journey.

My three children have been on journeys in their lives, and I've had the privilege of watching. I am so thankful for my great kids. Being a part of their lives from the day they were born through adulthood has been a blessing. With family, it's an emotional, relational journey.

We can go on career journeys, too. Soldiers know exactly what I'm talking about. The military doesn't ask their soldiers where they want to go. No, the military *tells* soldiers where they are going, sends them out and their journey begins. Their journey and experiences are part of a career path.

Sometimes people have an educational journey. A student goes to school for a particular degree to get the career they want; a two, four or six-year journey. Our education and career journeys become a story and a theme in our lives. I hope you see the pattern here.

Although less advantageous, we can even go on dark journeys. There are many dark journeys we stumble upon or choose to embark on.

Maybe a teenager starts drinking a little bit. Maybe you

took this kind of journey. We're hanging out with our friends and it's fun – good times and good laughs. But, pretty soon we're just drinking to get up in the morning and drinking at lunch time. All of a sudden, we're out of school carrying this journey forward. We're starting to show up for work late and starting to leave early. We're starting to make poor decisions with our money. Next thing you know, we're not drinking for fun, we're just drinking to drink and to get through. Now, our whole life starts getting sabotaged. This journey subtracts from our life. We started down a dark journey that's robbed our career. It's robbed our vitality. It's robbed our relationships.

Or, maybe we get caught up in meeting somebody at the office, and we start a little emotional journey with someone we're not married to. Then comes the adrenaline, the excitement of a new relationship; this clandestine relationship. Excitement and little thrills get going, and then we start crossing boundaries. At some point, the involvement brings shame, becoming toxic to our soul. The journeys down dark paths always end somewhere you don't want to be.

Everybody is on a journey of some kind, and I want to make this statement to you:

The most important journey that you will ever go on, the spiritual one, is a journey that will change your life.

To successfully go on a spiritual journey, you're going to need to learn and prepare yourself for it by learning to soak in God's presence. Yes, learn to soak in God's presence.

But, soaking... what exactly is it? Scripture says, "You'll show me the path." In other words, a spiritual journey is a journey of discovery. We spend time with Him, and He helps us discover His paths, His ways, His plans, His desires.

How many people would like to move into their future with clarity of thought and clarity of mind? What if you had an understanding of what your purpose in life is? The Bible says each of us has been created for good works. You were created for a good purpose! God wants you to know what it is. Knowing *what* you're created for is a journey of discovery. It's the journey to experience His presence and joy forevermore. It's the ability to get into His presence.

Do you realize it doesn't matter what happens in the stock market? It doesn't matter what happened at the office. It doesn't matter what the doctor's report is. You have the ability along this journey to say, "God I'm going to get in Your presence right now."

There's a peace that surpasses all understanding, and it's not based on what's going on externally around you. Consider this: I watch football games, and my team doesn't always win. Some people live their lives based on external circumstances; circumstances beyond their control. *My team lost. Now I'm unhappy. Happiness comes from what's outside of me.* Hello somebody!

If the home team loses, there are people who are

devastated, having a two, three, four, five, six-day moping session because their external source did not provide them joy. Don't get me wrong, I'm a sports fan who gets excited when my team wins and possibly a little bummed out if we don't win, but it doesn't determine my joy level. A sports game isn't real living. It's just an emotional moment in life. That source of entertainment has absolutely nothing to do with the valuable, spiritual journey we're on.

Life can get me down, but learning how to be in His presence gets me up. Did you catch that? You can learn how to enter into His presence. That is an essential life skill.

If I get a bad report, *okay, I need to get in His presence to get up.* If I have a financial hardship coming, *I need to get in His presence.* Relationship challenges? *I need to get in His presence. I need to get up.* And, in His presence is fullness of joy.

As a leader, I must know how to get myself up; how to get myself inspired. Leaders know how to get themselves inspired and not wait for inspiration. It's a journey of intimacy by God's side. Are you ready?

Come with me as I share thoughts, ideas and stories about taking a journey with God and soaking in His presence.

EMOTIONS

Most people, instead of making smart decisions, make emotional decisions. At the root of why we do what we do, people tend to make decisions based on where they can find comfort or pleasure of some kind. *Well, I'm not happy with my job, so I need to find another one that will make me happy...*

Emotions are a big part of who we are, and they can lead us astray at times. But as God's people, we know that in His presence is the fullness of joy and at His right hand are pleasures forevermore. *With* Him. In relationship with Him is pleasure.

Some people don't recognize that aspect of a Christian life. Yes, we live a life of sacrifice and discipline, but there are also great pleasures in God. There are pleasures that money can't buy. God will help you have money, but money in and of itself is not a pleasure. It's a piece of paper. It's a tool. When money becomes a pleasure, it will rob you of God.

I want you to deeply understand this: God wants you to have pleasure in your life. In fact, remember that God is even the author and creator of sex, but most people mess it up and follow the world's ways. Hello somebody! God is all about pleasure, and if you understand how to be in relationship with Him and how to do things His way, He will fill your life with the pleasure of His presence and with purpose.

FOREVERMORE

I love the phrase *forevermore*. Forever, more. It tells me that when you get to forever, there's more. When you get to the end, there's more. When you've got all that you want, there's still more. When you've lived life to the fullest, there's heaven. When you've had a great life here on earth, there's eternity. There's forever, and then more.

I love that about God. Believe Him when He says, "I have come to give you life and to give it more abundantly." It means He gives an abundantly overflowing life. He will open the windows of heaven for you and pour out blessings. So many blessings in fact, there will not be room enough to receive them.

That's overflow!

MORE MATURITY

Some people imagine that having more than they can handle would be fun. Well, having more than we can handle certainly requires that we mature!

For example, children can fill up your cup really fast and cause a young woman to turn into a mature woman real fast. It'll take a young boy and turn him into a man. Children make you grow up, because the blessing of God will mature you. It either matures you or you can allow it to overwhelm you.

God has blessed you, but be careful that you don't curse that blessing. Instead, mature with it. God may have blessed your life with a great relationship, but if you don't mature with it and you remain selfish, it will feel like a burden.

NEVER ALONE

Psychologists have said loneliness is the number one psychological disorder in the world even though we're closer in physical proximity than ever before. We live in apartments, go to clubs, have hundreds of friends on social media, but still we are lonely. We're in marriages and we are lonely. Children feel lost in families. Divorces break families down. Many feel so displaced. For the most part, our culture does not promote multi-generational living, where people would have the support of multiple generations surrounding them. People can feel really disconnected and very alone.

Most of the depression people deal with, much of the displacement people deal with, much of the sense of abandonment people deal with is a lack of feeling connected. But, there is Someone to connect with, and He's always available. *By Your side, Lord, in Your presence, intimacy with You.* In His presence, for the rest of my life, I don't have to be alone.

Even when I'm alone it's some of the best times of my life. Why? Because I'm not lonely. I'm with Him, and in His presence I have fellowship and dialogue with my God. I have instant connection. You, too, can live each day with a deep, meaningful connection. Come on somebody!

THIS DAY

Let me say about this journey, you're never too young to start and you're never too old to begin. Somebody is thinking, "Well, my life is passing by." Please don't tell yourself that. Every time you say *my life is passing me by* you've just wasted another day. Every time you say *I've missed out on life, I've made so many bad choices*...it means you're choosing not to live today. The past is simply replaying, again.

"This is the day the Lord has made; we will rejoice and be glad in it" (Psalm 118:24).

The only day you will ever have is today. You've got to be able to say, "I will start today." Today is the acceptable time. The Bible says, "Today is the day of salvation." All you get is one day at a time, and you don't even get a whole day. You get a minute; this minute. All you have is this moment. What you do with right now matters.

You're never too old to begin and you're never too young to start this thing called a spiritual journey. It is the most important journey you will ever make. It is the journey of a lifetime. You will have stories to tell for the rest of your life. You will have experiences that will stay with you for eternity.

GROWING ON A JOURNEY

This journey that I'm inviting you to go on, is one that we can travel together. Let's go together as the body of Christ. But, whether you go on the journey with me or not, as a pastor, it is my calling to go.

Growth is a great alienator. Here's what often happens: there's a couple who aren't plugged in to God and don't go to church, they don't honor God with their income, and don't serve in God's church. And then, guess what? One of them surrenders their life to God. They start coming to church and want to start serving and volunteering. And, they want to start tithing and giving money to the church. It's a situation I've seen many times. That will create jealousy in the person who is not making the journey.

And, if the other person doesn't take the journey, you know what they're going to want you to do? *Don't give that money to that church. Don't spend so much time in that church. Why are you going to church so much?* They will try to hold you back because they don't want to make the journey with you. We often compromise going on the journey because we think *I want peace with that person more than peace with my God.*

There may be tension created by going on the journey... but go anyway. Still love those who won't come along with you. If you're in that kind of conflicting relationship, when you go home and your spouse gets mad at you for going to church, just love them. Just give

17

them a big hug. Just give them a big ol' wet kiss. Just say, "I was thinking about you in church today." Use church as the reason to connect, not resist. "I was in church today and it made me want to come home, hug all up with you and love on you." In that case, they'll be wanting you to go to church! "When are you going to church again? Because every time you go to church, life is better for me." Try it! Maybe they'll even want to check this church thing out for themselves.

"You will show me the path of life; in Your presence is fullness of joy; at Your right hand are pleasures forevermore." Psalm 16:11

GROW TOGETHER

I often tell my pastors and teams, "As much as I love you, if you don't grow with me, we will grow apart."

I'll also tell my team, "You know who gets me the best? People who are brand new. *You* get the pastor you think you know, but I'm a growing pastor. And, if all you know is the pastor you knew a year ago or five years ago, you don't know the pastor today. You're looking at me through the lenses of history versus looking at me through the lenses of how I'm growing in God today. The people who don't have a history with me hear me with fresh ears, but others may still view me through old lenses. That's a brilliant thought, by the way. Keep that perspective for anyone you know who is growing.

My staff and team understand that concept and we talk about it together. But, what about us as a church family? Or, even your family? What are you hearing? What are you seeing? What are you sensing? How have you advanced?

We have to go on the journey together, because if it's not together, it will be alone or not at all. I've decided to go. If I don't go on the journey, then life becomes all about *I'm done. Where's the rapture? Let's get out of here. To hell with everybody else,* literally. That's the wrong perspective. I will not live that way.

I invite you to go on this journey. As God's church, let's go together. In 2 Chronicles 15, there was a king by the name of Asa who wanted to bring spiritual revival to the nation. The nation had gotten far from God and he wanted to restore them. It says they gathered the leaders and the people in the community, and they entered a covenant to seek the Lord God of their fathers with all their heart and with all their souls. He said, "Let's go on this journey together."

Let me ask you this question: Thirty years from now, do you think the current players on your favorite sports team will still be there? Will they be playing anymore? How many know in 30 years they're probably going to be carrying some extra weight? In 30 years they may have some muscles and bones that don't work real well. They'll retire and spread out all over the nation, but should they ever have a cup of coffee or a dinner or a visit with their former teammates, do you think they will reminisce about the season of the journey they went on together?

Do you think they'll bring up the memorable moments? "Remember that one play we made? Remember that comeback we had? Do you remember that catch you made? You remember you knocked that guy out? Yeah, we did that. You remember..."? Yes they will. They'll have great stories to tell because they went on a journey together.

It's the same for us. We will have big memories and stories to tell. We'll remember that one place we were at together. But, if we stay behind, we'll not experience the next level. We'll just watch it. In that case, we'll just watch somebody else live their journey and ride the emotional roller coaster of watching somebody else win in life.

Why don't *you* start winning in life, and then watch what happens. Somebody's going to follow your story.

INSPIRED HEART

Jesus wants you to have life and have it more abundantly. He wants you to know the peace and the joy of His presence and the intimacy that comes from having a relationship with Him. You're going to start winning in life and people are going to start watching you and following you because Jesus said, "Follow me and I will make you fishers of men." When you start following Christ, others are going to start following you because God will cause you to live an inspired life.

Nobody wants to follow an uninspired person. If you want a great marriage, be an inspired spouse. It's true! Let me share one verse from Psalm 27. "When you said seek my face, my heart said to you, your face Lord will I seek." Here's the question: When I say to you, "Let's go on a spiritual journey," be honest with yourself. Do you want to go? What does your heart say? Does it say, "Really, I just want to hear a nice message and then be on my way."

When you're invited to go, what does your heart say? Does your heart say, "You know, I'm going to get around to it. I'm going to start. I'm going to really go places in God. I promise I'll do that... tomorrow." You put it off, postpone it. You procrastinate. Or, you say, "You know what? I've just got too many other interests. I'm too busy. I'm enjoying my life too much right now," and if we're honest, "I'm really just not that interested in making an investment of my time, my emotion and my thought-life into a discovery of a relationship. I just don't have time to do this thing and I'm really not interested."

See, people don't go on journeys because they're just not interested in going. I got invited to fly on a cargo plane once, and I said, "You know, not interested." I thought about it. I prayed about it for a minute. But nope, not interested. I had the invitation, but it was something I just didn't want to do.

I don't know why you go to church, but I hope you attend for more than just hearing a sermon or a message, or to see a friend, to talk, or to laugh. I pray that it's something more than that. I hope you are looking for a spiritual journey. This spiritual journey is highly personal, but can be shared with others.

PREPARE

There are certain journeys I'm just not interested in taking. There are plenty of options I could choose, but some journeys won't help my life in any way. A spiritual journey, however, is vital to my soul.

To be honest, unfortunately some people are not interested in a spiritual journey. Not only do they not want to go, but they'll make fun of you for taking it. They'll criticize you for taking that step. They think you're weird for your pursuit of God. But, to *not* pursue God is a regrettable decision, because everything comes out of our inner man – our spirit and soul – and the one journey that often gets neglected by most people is the journey of the spirit.

When I say, "Prepare your heart," what does your heart say to you? Are you excited? If you get the journey of the spirit right, your relationships will be right. Your life will be good.

The other day my wife came to me, and we were comparing calendars and making some plans. I had something I was planning and getting excited about, and she looked at me and said, "You need to look at the calendar again, because I have plans for you that week."

First, we had a moment of intense conversation. Then, I realized she was right and I was wrong. I went back and made some phone calls to clear my calendar. Hers was a better offer. With her it was going to be a better journey.

Are you catching this? I had to prepare myself to go on the journey. You've got to prepare yourself to go on this journey with God.

There's an incredible promise for you in Jeremiah 33:3. It says, "Call to me and I will answer you, I will tell you marvelous and wonderful things that you would never figure out on your own." God says, "If you call to me I will answer you and will reveal marvelous things. You will never figure this out without seeking me."

CAUTION

There's a warning for us about not seeking God. In 2 Chronicles, another king named Rehoboam "did evil because he did not prepare his heart to seek God." Listen to this carefully. This is the warning, and you may not like it:

If you do not prepare your heart to seek God, you are preparing to do evil.

If you are not preparing to seek God, you are preparing to sabotage your life. If you're not preparing to seek God, you're preparing to miss your destiny. If you're not preparing to seek God, you're preparing to miss what you were created for. If you're not preparing to seek God, you're preparing to miss the whole reason of why you are on this planet. From God's perspective, it would be evil for you to miss out on the incredible plan He has for you.

As we can see, a spiritual journey is something to prepare for. It doesn't come naturally for us. We have to be intentional about it, and that requires some of our time and attention.

SOAK IT

I want to introduce this thought of what it really means to *SOAK*. What does this really mean: *to go on a spiritual journey I have to soak?*

To soak is the process of prolonged immersion to soften. Have you ever noticed that something hard, placed into the right environment for an extended period of time, can go from hard to soft, because of the new environment? Oh, that's a really good thought.

I asked my wife a cooking question: "Kelly, when you cook beans, how long do they have to soak before they're ready? An hour? Overnight? I have no idea." She gave me my bean answer, and she added, "But, you can do it the fast way." "What's that?" I wondered. She said, "You can boil water, put it in there while it's steaming and put the lid on it." Oh, that's perfect. That's where most people are at. Most people do not seek God until they have no other options, until they're in the hot water.

God I need you now. Do it quick. Come on God. God I'm soft. I'm defenseless. I'm broken God! Oh God do it now!

That's the way most people get softened up to accept what God has to offer, right? That's the way most people soak. They get their life so hot and in so much turmoil, they don't have anything else they can do, and no other place they can turn. Here's good news: it doesn't always have to be in boiling water that we soak. Come on somebody!

How many know sometimes you cannot put the dish into the dishwasher until it's been soaked a while? Some people don't want to wait for it to be soaked, so what do they do? They scrub it. They scrub it hard. *I'll scrub that off myself.* That's what some of us try to do to other people. *I see that stain on you. I see that hard spot on you. We got to scrub it. I'll fix you!*

I used to try to do that as a young pastor. I wore myself out and made people mad at me. There's so much friction going on. *You need to change. You need to change. Well, you're bossy.* Sometimes we try to get someone else cleaned up faster than they want to be cleaned. I finally figured out people need to soak in God a while, and then their stains just wipe off; they just fall off.

Our hearts need to soak to soften. Soaking is going to give you a new heart. It will give you new strength.

Some of you have hard hearts because you went through a divorce. Your heart's so shut down, and you're living lonely. It doesn't mean that God wouldn't have something for you, but you're stuck in your hurt. Listen to me. You've got to let God heal that so you're free to move forward in life.

Some of you feel dirty. You feel ashamed. You feel embarrassed. You've done dumb stuff. If you will go soak in God's presence and promises, that guilt, shame and embarrassment will start washing off of you.

Some of you got hurt in church and you're so hardened. *I'll never get involved in church again. I'll never trust again.*

You just need that stuff washed off. You need to soak. You've got to prepare for the journey.

SATURATE UNTIL SATISFIED

Soaking is a process. It's to saturate completely; to saturate completely by absorption until no more can be held. Think of a sponge. A sponge is bone dry, until you put it on a liquid and it'll suck it up until it can't suck up anymore. Take some time to soak in all you can contain. Allow yourself to slow down and breathe. But, do you want to? My question to you is how hungry is your heart?

The first scripture I ever learned as a believer was Matthew 5 verse 6: Blessed are those who hunger and thirst after righteousness, for they shall be filled. I realized that I've got to bring the hunger in order to be fed. The reality is some of us are just not hungry enough. We don't have an appetite for this thing. The appetite for more of God doesn't happen automatically – you've got to create the appetite, purposefully. The thing about appetites is at first you might not want to eat your vegetables, but appetites can grow.

To soak means to be saturated until satisfied. Yes, saturate until satisfied. God is saying that if you'll hunger and thirst after His righteousness, you'll be filled to satisfaction. But, here's the thing: I've got to bring the hunger, He brings the supply. When I'm satisfied, the feeding stops. Keep bringing the hunger and don't be satisfied after just a few drops.

When I was a kid, I experimented with cigarettes a couple times. Maybe you did, too, or you continue to smoke now. Remember the first time you tried it? It was horrible. The first time you smoke a cigarette, there's no way you like it. There's absolutely no way you like that first drag on a cigarette. You got dizzy. Smoke got in your eyes and burned your throat. You're coughing, but you're going to try and be cool about it. You're going to smoke through this pain and disgust. And, you force yourself to go back again for seconds.

Pretty soon, if you keep it up, an addiction starts. You actually create a desire for it. After a while, that desire turns into an intense craving, and you've got to have one in the morning when you get up. *Got to have my smoke to get started.* You've got to have one when you go to bed. *I'm about to go to bed, I need a smoke.*

Then you're at the office and you have a little conflict with a co-worker. *I've got to go outside and have me a smoke. I can't take it in here no more.* You start having to smoke. You took something that was horrible and turned it into an incredible craving. What if we, instead, create cravings for good things?

As a young man, I had no idea that I would be a pastor. I got an intense craving for God, but pastoring was never attractive to me, until I started tasting and seeing that He was good.

Under the Influence

What you crave and take into yourself influences you. To saturate means to become intoxicated, or filled. In Old English, when a person became drunk, they were called a "sop" or a "soaker." They're pickled!

When a person is intoxicated, it means there is a diminishment of their physical and mental capacities. How many know that when you soak in God's presence, you will come under the influence?

When you come under the influence of alcohol you talk funny. When you come under the influence of God you talk funny, too. You might start talking in tongues and people might say, "Oh, you're crazy." Well, listen to an intoxicated person talk. How do *they* sound? Not very coherent, logical or rational.

People somehow think they can drive a car under the influence of alcohol. Some even think they do life better intoxicated. I used to play sports with people, and they thought if they smoked a few joints before the game, they played better. They really believed stuff like that! It didn't help them play better, but probably they just noticed their errors less! You know people like that too; people who do crazy stuff and think they're better. But no, being intoxicated or under the influence of drugs and alcohol puts you in a diminished capacity.

But, when you get under the Spirit of God, you get under the influence of a different kind and you prophesy. To prophesy means to speak under the influence of God. You see visions, which is to see by faith; to see under the influence of God.

STEEP

Miss Kelly, my wife, loves tea. To release its full flavor, tea is one of those drinks that needs time to sit before you can drink it. Likewise, to soak means to steep something until the extraction of its essence.

It's the idea of taking a tea bag and steeping (soaking) it in hot water until what's in it is saturated and released into the surrounding water, altering its flavor. You may not realize it yet, but you have gifts and talents that have been given to you by God. There's something that's in you. These gifts are "without repentance," meaning God's not going to take them from you. However, they may never be released.

A tea bag, unless it gets in hot water, never releases its content. Unless you get in the right environment, you're not going to release your content. It's the extraction of the essence that's in you. You are created for a good work, but if you don't get in the right environment, you're not going to release what you were created for. You're not going to release the gift that's in you. You won't discover what that good work is.

The Bible says that you and I are the workmanship of God created in Christ Jesus for good works which he prepared before the foundation of time. There are things in you that you were created for that you will never release, like a teabag, until you enter the process of soaking. You will never release what you were created for until you start soaking in God's presence.

PRECIOUS TREASURE

If you don't *SOAK* in God's presence and release your gift, release your talent, release the treasure that is in you, something precious is lost. The Bible says, "We have this treasure of ministry in earthen vessels that the glory and the excellence will not be of us but would be of God." Do you understand what I'm trying to say? There's something in you that wants to be released out of you. You might say, "I'm a mess. I'm just an earthen vessel. There can't be anything good in here."

When Paul was writing and referring to earthen vessels having treasure in them, in that time period, earthen vessels were clay pots. They were common, everyday, household Tupperware. Many plastic food containers go bad pretty quick, right? The idea isn't to wrestle with it and try to save it for ten years. The idea is just to use it a short while and throw it away. When the lid gets warped and doesn't close anymore, throw it away. When you left it in the microwave too long, throw it away. When it gets stained by spaghetti sauce, throw it away. You see the whole idea of Tupperware is to throw it away because it's cheap. Clay pots were chapel-ware.

Watch this. How many know that if there's treasure *in* the Tupperware you don't throw the Tupperware away? There's a treasure in you. While you may be a *crackpot*... there's treasure in you. When you get in the environment of God, all your true essence will start being released out of you. It's going to extract the essence in you to bring it out of you. To soak is to be softened, to absorb and release. So, soften, absorb and release what God has for you.

RELATIONSHIP

How do we discover our purpose in God, how do we experience His presence, and how do we have an intimate relationship with Him?

When I say an intimate relationship with God, that might not necessarily be attractive to some people. As I mentioned before, psychologists say that loneliness is the number one disorder in the world right now. It's the root of depression, suicide, addiction and many kinds of negative behavior. We live in more physical proximity than any other point in history, yet we are lonely in our hearts.

What would it mean to you to live your life without feeling disconnected? What would it mean to live your life not feeling lost, not feeling like you don't fit in, not feeling like you don't belong? What would it feel like to feel special? All of that comes out of an intimate connection and relationship with God – the one who is faithful and never lets you down.

S = SEEK

To help you remember how to soak, I am introducing *SOAK* as an acronym. If you'll learn and remember what the letters stand for, it will help you succeed. First, "S" is to *seek* God; to *seek* to know Him.

TIME

Beginning the journey, the spiritual journey to seek God, is the most important decision you will ever make in your life. Listen carefully. To make the decision to seek God does not require money, it does not require education, nor does it require opportunity or connection. It just requires something we're all given and that's called *time*.

Have you ever noticed when it comes to time, we all have an equal amount of it: 24 hours in a day. And really, all we have a grasp on is *this* moment. We never really know how much time we have on this earth, so that's why we make the most of each moment.

You and I possess time – it's a resource we each have. Just pause and think about this. The decision that you're about to make, or maybe you've already started, is a decision I want to encourage you forward in. It is so simple. It's the decision to begin seeking.

Let Him know, say this prayer: God, I want to seek You, and I make the decision to seek You from this moment on.

THE FIRST STEP

Making the decision to seek God is an easy one, but at the same time it's the toughest decision you'll ever make. How many would be honest that some of the hardest things you've ever done in your life was just to *begin*? The first step of something is the hardest. For me, getting to church the first time was the hardest. Tithing for the very first time was the hardest. When I lifted my hand and said, "Jesus, be Lord of my life," the first time was the hardest. Forgiving somebody for the first time was the hardest. Releasing control and truly trusting God for the first time was the hardest.

The reason it's difficult is because it's the decision to break the inertia in our life. It's the decision to break the stagnation, compromise and the luke-warmness in our life. It's the decision to begin.

As a pastor, one of my biggest concerns is that people attend church, they sit and they listen, but never engage. **If you never engage God for yourself, you'll never go on the journey. If you never go on the journey of seeking God, you'll miss your destiny.**

HIS FACE

Psalm 27:8 says, "When You said, 'Seek My face,' my heart said to You, 'Your face, Lord, I will seek.'" I love that scripture. When God says to you, "Seek My face," the Psalmist's heart replied, "Lord, Your face, I will seek." What does *your* heart say?

Many people tell me they're trying to find themselves, trying to find their purpose and trying to find who they are. Stop! Stop trying to find *you*, and start seeking *Him*. Your life is found in Him.

Maybe that's the word of the Lord to you today: *today is the day to begin. Today is the day to start. Today is the first day of the rest of a different kind of life.* Today is the day to say, "Yes, I will seek my God." I will lose myself in the journey of seeking Him, and He promised us that if we lose ourselves seeking Him, we will find ourselves. You can't find yourself until you lose yourself.

Some of the most confused people I've ever met are people who are *trying to find themselves*. Some of the most clear-headed people I've ever met are people who have lost themselves. An addict is a clear-headed, singularly-focused person. They're very clear. *I want my high. I will steal from you. I will rob from you to get my high.* They've lost themselves in what they seek. In losing themselves, they have found an identity; unfortunately a negative identity.

When you seek God, you seek His presence and you find

your identity. Seeking Him does not have a negative consequence. He does not forsake those who seek Him.

YOU WILL FIND

Psalm chapter 9 verse 10 says, – "Lord, You've never forsaken those who seek You."

Pause and think about that. Do you hear what Scripture is saying to you? God has never forsaken those who seek Him. It will never be a waste of your time to seek Him. You will never be disappointed seeking Him. You will never be put to shame seeking Him. You will never be embarrassed seeking Him. God says, "You will never be forsaken." In Isaiah, He says, "I did not say to the seed of Jacob, 'Seek Me in vain.'" God promised that when we seek, we shall also find.

I'm excited for you. I'm excited for your journey. The Holy Spirit is excited about this journey, but I cannot want something for you more than you want it for yourself. The desire and decision to seek God has got to be your decision.

Grab hold of this promise out of Jeremiah 29 verse 13, "You will seek Me and find Me when you search for Me with all your heart."

Do you hear what God is saying? God is saying, "When you seek Me with all that is in you, you will find Me. When you take Me seriously, you're taking your life seriously. When you take seeking Me seriously, you take your destiny seriously. When you take seeking Me seriously, you take your purpose seriously."

One of the most familiar verses in the Bible is Jeremiah 29:11, "'For I know the thoughts that I think toward you,' says the Lord, 'thoughts of peace and not of evil, to give you a future and a hope.'" That's good news to be excited about!

CONSECRATED

How do I explain to you the gift of a purpose? How do I explain to you the feeling that you're not alone and you're connected? How do I explain to you what it is to know; that God is *for* you and not against you? How do I explain to you what it means to feel special? How do I explain these to you? As part of the promise, you will know and understand these things if you'll go on the journey of seeking Him and soaking in Him. God's going to do amazing things in your life.

When you declare, "God, I want to really take these things seriously and seek You," you are consecrating yourself to the Lord. To consecrate yourself means to set apart as belonging to God; "God, I'm going to dedicate this to you and set this apart for You. This (time, heart, money, child, business, etc.) is going to belong to You."

Consecration is always the catalyst for every great spiritual awakening in your life. Every spiritual surge, every growth spurt that occurs in your life will be on the heels of a season of consecration. In other words, you're setting something aside to belong to him.

Consecration may seem like one of those old, biblical vocabulary words. It just means setting something apart to belong to God. Whatever you consecrate, you're making it holy, you're making it sacred, you're making it special and you're setting it apart to belong to God. Consecration is always the catalyst. It's the genesis. It's the beginning.

Here's what Joshua said to the people in the book of Joshua 3:5 "Consecrate yourself, for tomorrow the Lord will do amazing things with you." The genesis, catalyst or the beginning is always consecration, but the end is always amazing. The end of seeking God is always a "Wow! That's awesome. That is truly awesome. That is beyond description." He will show you amazing things.

Today, consecrate yourself; tomorrow, wonderful things. He would say to us, "Today, set time aside to seek Me. Tomorrow amazing things start coming into your life, alignment starts coming into your life, gifts start coming into your life. You start absorbing who I am. You start releasing who you are. Amazing."

NO BOREDOM

Listen. There's a warning. If you do not practice this thing called consecration, the choices are either consecration or boredom. If you do not consecrate yourself to seek God, you will get bored with spirituality. But, boredom does not lead to *boring*...let me explain what I mean.

I, myself, might be boring at times, but I do not have boredom in my life. I enjoy moments of being boring and taking it easy, but experiencing boredom means I've taken time that belongs to God and have wasted it. If I'm not consecrating myself to God, I will wander into a dark journey. Idle hands often find trouble. Boredom, if it's not changed to consecration, means wasted potential and possible harm.

In 2 Chronicles chapter 12, God's people "entered into a covenant to seek the Lord the God of their fathers with all their hearts." That's the beginning of every genesis. They entered a covenant to seek God. Three chapters later, and under a new leader who didn't honor the covenant, 2 Chronicles 15:12 refers to Rehoboam and it says, "He did evil because he did not prepare his heart to seek the Lord."

Remember the lesson Rehoboam had to learn: if you don't prepare your heart to seek God, you'll be preparing to do evil. Rehoboam had a destiny. Rehoboam had a calling. Rehoboam had a purpose, but he did not prepare his heart to seek God. As a result, it led him to do evil. His life could have been different.

If you don't prepare your heart to seek God, you're going to mess up your life. Don't get mad at me for saying that. Put your rotten tomatoes away! It's just the truth of it. You'll mess up your marriage. You'll mess up your finances. You'll mess up your family. You'll mess up your health. You'll mess up your body. You will mess up your life if you do not prepare your heart to seek God. That's just the way it is.

SETTING ASIDE

What does it really look like to consecrate yourself? Let's break it down a little bit further. To consecrate yourself is to prepare by setting aside. It's taking something and setting it aside for God. The most important thing that you can take and set aside for God is *time*.

Sometimes, I'll come into the kitchen and Kelly will be cooking all kinds of food, and *none* of it is for me. This happens especially at Christmas time! Christmas cookies and breads, birthday cakes, a potluck dish for a party – you get the idea. It gets prepared and set aside for somebody else. Are you catching this?

You see, when you consecrate something, you're saying, "God, I'm taking some time out of my life. I'm taking some time and I will set it aside. I'm going to prepare it for You, and it no longer belongs to me." That dedicated time no longer belongs to me. This time becomes a consecrated time; a holy time. This is a special time. *This is Your time God. I'm recognizing this as Your time.*

If you know me, you know I love football. For the longest time, my Sunday mornings were consecrated to the NFL, not God. Thankfully, that's not how I live my life anymore. God has a destiny and a good plan for me, for my Sunday mornings, rather than sitting watching someone else's destiny. A lot more people would be sitting at home on Sunday mornings if it wasn't set aside as God's time, and vice versa. Many others would be coming to church if that time wasn't set aside for football.

It's real common to take what is holy and give it to something that is not holy. Something not holy doesn't necessarily mean it's evil, but it's not holy. And so, in the case of time that *was* holy, we take what was holy and we give it to something that isn't. If you're going to seek God, give Him some time. Take time somewhere in your schedule and give it to Him and say, "God, this is Your time."

QUIET TIME

There's a curious scripture in Revelation chapter 8. It says, "When the angel opened the 7th seal... " I love this, "... there was silence in heaven for about half an hour." If you read Revelation, there's a lot of shouting, thunder and lightning. It's roaring, and there's singing with loud voices. Then, all of a sudden in this chapter, a half hour silence occurs.

What would you do with a half hour in God's presence? What if it was that simple to say, "God, I'm going to consecrate a half hour out of every day to soak in Your presence. This half hour is for You." Well, it is that easy!

Jesus, in the Garden of Gethsemane, asked His disciples for an hour to pray. Negotiate time with God. Start small if you need to. Here's the key: schedule it, set it aside and say, "God, this is Yours. This no longer belongs to me. This is Yours, and I'm going to seek You."

You may be thinking, *I set aside time for God...then what?* There are a lot of creative ways to spend time with God. Here are some of the things I do during my soaking time. I have used prayer outlines. Sometimes I sit in amazement about His blessings, and I just take it all in. Also, counting the many ways I am grateful to God helps me express my heart to Him. *God, I'm so grateful. God, I'm just grateful. You love me. You saved me, chose me, blessed me.* I could spend a whole lot of time talking about everything I'm grateful for.

In fact, gratefulness is the protocol for coming into His presence. We enter His courts with praise and into His presence with thanksgiving. This is a great place to start soaking: "God, I'm just going to practice gratitude."

At other times during my quiet time with God, I start unloading all of my cares because He cares for me. I often wonder how people take the weariness, the stresses, the struggles, problems and difficulties and take all of it into their soul without a way to unload it. They've never taken the opportunity and said, "God, I had this hurt," or, "God, I have this struggle," or, "God, I have this concern," or, "God, I have this weight,' or, "God, my kids, my relationships, my life and my finances... " and say, "Here it is, God." Everyone needs to understand they can go to God and say, "I'm seeking You, and I'm going to unload to You this heavy thing I'm carrying... "

Sometimes, it's petitions. The Bible says, "Let your petitions be known to God." Petitions are the things I'm wanting, believing for, desiring, etc.

I love reading scripture in my soaking time, and as I read, I dialogue with God. I read scripture slowly. There was a time in my life when I read a lot of verses and chapters every day. Now, I read much more slowly. When I read scriptures at a slower pace, at this phase in my life, it gives me more opportunity to dialogue with God. *Hmmm...that's interesting.* I'll write notes and capture thoughts.

One of the most important things I do in my time with

God is interceding for the needs of others. There are many ways to engage God during your time with Him.

HOLY TIME

In school, I had a professor tell me that if a person studies a subject for an hour a day, within 3 years they'll be a local expert. Research and learn about something for one hour a day for 5 years, and in 5 years you'll be a regional expert. And, in 7 years you would be a national expert. That thought has stuck with me all these years. You see, if you start seeking God, there's a compound effect. It will grow in you.

There's no magic formula with God. You and God can negotiate time. It's just critical that you make the time, that you schedule the time, and that you set it aside and say, "God, this is Your time." If you gave God just a half hour a day, that's over 180 hours a year.

Consecrate yourself and get ready. *God, I'm preparing something for You.* You can certainly consecrate other things to him like your treasure and talent. But, most importantly, God wants your time. *I'm setting this aside. With this time, I will seek You.*

Next, pronounce it as holy. To consecrate means you've set it aside. To pronounce it as holy means *it belongs to You. I have separated it for you.* It's very important to recognize it as special, holy, belonging to God.

It's amazing what God can make holy. For Moses, it was bush, a section of ground, it was a rod, and at other times it was rock. God can take a common thing, like our lives, and make it holy.

You're Mine

When I was a young believer and first started living for God, I started seeking God, which caused me to separate from many unhealthy relationships. I was embracing this new life that God had called me to, and my exciting journey was beginning. But, my previous friends were not on the journey with me, and I remember feeling quite lonely. While lonely, I talked to God. Saying that seems like an oxymoron. Is it possible to be talking to God *and* be lonely? Yes, that's how I felt.

I vividly remember one day when I was at work. I was walking back to my work truck, feeling lonely. As I opened the door, I felt like the Holy Spirit said to me, "Look back." As I looked back, even though it was a summer day, it was almost like I could see where my feet had been. It reminded me of seeing footsteps through fresh snow. I didn't see it physically, but I'm under the influence. I'm seeing stuff. I'm seeing crazy stuff. My co-worker with me couldn't see it. Like Saul on the road to Damascus, I'm the only one seeing this.

I felt like God said to me, "Your life is now Mine, and it's holy to Me. It belongs to Me, and I'm putting you on a different path." God wants to take things that are common and make them holy. He told Moses, "Moses, take your shoes off." "Lord, it's a desert out here. There are rocks out here." "No, no. It is holy ground now." God takes common things and makes them uncommon when you declare they're holy.

Then, I'm sitting on my couch watching a Seahawk's game, wrestling with what's next on my path. I had the opportunity to participate in Christian leadership classes, and God was reminding me, "Do you remember that path I'm calling you on?" At this point, I have no idea I'm going to start a church. I don't know I'm going to become a pastor, but all of a sudden, I'm feeling God is speaking. "I want you to let this football thing go, and I want you to start going to Christian leadership classes," which were, of course, on Sunday afternoons. That was a big deal for me. I can look back now and see that it was either give up football for that time period, or give up (what I now know as) my calling.

Literally, it took me over a year before I said yes. I didn't say yes immediately. It's like, "God, You and I have a problem. You see, Sunday morning is Yours, Sunday afternoon is mine, because I want that time." God was asking for more of my time, and I had to give up something that was common to me (my time) and make it holy for Him.

It was still a bit of a struggle, because I'd get to watch the first quarter, maybe into the second quarter, then I'd have to leave and go to class. God was asking me to give Him time, pronouncing it holy. "This is holy. This belongs to God."

THE FIRST PORTION

God not only wants our time, but He also designed us with talents and abilities to be used for Him. When I hired our worship pastor, Trisha, I said, "Trisha, it's not just time that God desires, it's your talent and treasure as well." I went on, "Trisha, God has a plan for you, and I want to see it come out of you. I don't even know what all of that looks like yet, but there's a place within you that belongs to God. You already recognize that. God wants you to give that to Him, and I'm excited to see what happens when you do."

You know what I'm talking about. Sometimes people have talents, but they won't give them to God. They have great abilities, but they won't give them to God. They have valuable skills, but they won't give them to God. They have leadership ability, but they won't give it to God. They have influence, but they won't give it to God. They have abundant resources, but they won't give any to God. They won't call any of it holy and set it aside, or say, "This belongs to God," pronouncing that it's holy.

I encourage you to say yes to God and offer Him your time, your talent and your treasure. Consecrate it, proclaim it as holy, and then observe it. By *observe it*, I mean make the decision, take action and stick with it. You can say something is holy. You can set something aside, and then take it back for yourself.

The best example is the tithe. It's one thing to tithe once, but it's another thing to stick with it. Sometimes we start a journey and set something aside for God, then we change our mind. *Oh, never mind.*

Do you realize the first portion of your income is holy to God? Some people won't even do the initial step of consecrating it. *God I'm not even setting it aside. It's mine, not Yours.* Then, others say, "Yes, I recognize the first ten percent is God's," but they won't release it. They recognize it and even call it His, but don't actually observe or take action on it.

"For the Lord has never forsaken those who seek Him." Psalm 9:10

If I were to go back three decades ago and say, "No, God, I'm not going to give up my football time," I would not be helping God impact my community and you would not be my future. As hard as that decision was at the moment, now it's almost embarrassing to say it was a sacrifice, considering all I've gained in my life from it.

God, I don't feel I'm that smart, but thank you I wasn't stupid. Thank you for being patient. I did put You off for a year. Thank you for being patient with me. I started with consecrating some time.

Next, I moved on to consecrating other aspects of my life. What would happen in my life and finances, if I took what was God's and gave it away to frivolous spending? What would happen if I took the gift to lead, communicate and influence and used it to manipulate or control? What would happen if I took what was holy and gave it to something unholy?

Matthew chapter 7 speaks about this. In verse 6, Jesus says, "Do not give what is holy to the dogs; nor cast your pearls before swine, lest they trample them under their feet, and turn and tear you in pieces." That verse talks about trying to teach unteachable people, but it also refers to taking what's holy and casting it to something unholy.

If I take what belongs to God and don't seek Him with it, I will always regret it. If I take what belongs to God and don't serve Him with it, I'll always regret it. If I take what belongs to God and use it for something other than seeking and serving Him, it will always turn on me. I'll always regret it. I'll always be disappointed.

Count on this: the result of consecration is always awe.

O = OBSERVE

If you are a person who says you love God, is there genuine expression of that love in your life? Plenty of people say, "Oh, I don't believe in God, and I don't believe in the church." They have a big opinion about something they know little about. Think about that. They have a big opinion about something they have not investigated, they've not researched, they've not studied, or they may have some experiences, but they have not really gone through the journey. But, for those of us on the journey, there ought to be an outward expression, or proof, of our walk with God.

This leads me to the next letter in our *SOAK* acronym – "O." O is for *observe* His promptings. Yes, observe His (sometimes crazy) promptings! The blessing is not in hearing only – the blessing comes through engaging. When you engage, that's when the difference begins. Engage in this process, and learn to observe His promptings.

CAN I KNOW YOU?

The good news is the journey of *SOAK* does not require you to start with faith. It just requires you start to seek to know Him. Honestly, you can't love Him until you know Him. Seek first. *God, are You really there? Are You really true? Can I really trust You? What does Your Word really say? What are you really like?*

Then, you begin to know Him. **When you know Him, you cannot help but love him.** Loving Him leads to falling in love with Him and serving Him. This is where observing comes in.

Sometimes we're trying to get people to serve God that don't yet love God. To know Him, the true Him, is to love Him. If you get people to know God, they fall in love with God, and have no problem serving Him. Then, they want to serve His family, share His love and share with His family. Interestingly, in the serving of God, we begin to discover who we are, because we'll never find ourselves until we serve Him.

Know ⟶ **love** ⟶ **serve** ⟶ **discover purpose**

In discovering who I am, I experience His presence, His power, His grace, His miracles, His Spirit, and what it means to be *living my faith*. I don't have to start with faith. I just have to start with a genuine question. *Can I know You?*

Living your faith, doing something about what you've discovered while seeking, is where you start observing.

OBSERVATION TIME

After Moses died, God gave Joshua special instructions (Joshua 1:8): "This Book of the Law shall not depart from your mouth, but you shall meditate in it day and night, that you may observe to do according to all that is written in it." Wow. We must take the time. If you know anything about Joshua, when Moses would go to seek the Lord outside of the camp, Joshua would go with him. Joshua was the *only one* who would go with him. Even when Moses was done, the Bible says that Joshua would stay longer and soak in God's presence.

It's interesting that when Moses was dead, the only person God could find to give direction to was the person who was seeking Him. Some people don't really experience God's direction and God's leadership in their lives because He's waiting for their attention. God is waiting to get our attention.

"You shall meditate in it day and night that you may observe… " You may observe. You may observe, "…to do according to all that is written in it." It goes on to say, "For then you will make your way prosperous, and then you will have good success."

Looking for prosperity? Looking for good success? Observe God's leadership in your life.

Prosperity isn't always about money. Success isn't always about a position. Sometimes you want to prosper in relationships, prosper in family and in a career.

Money is simply a tool to help you get where you want to go in life. God has no problem giving you the tool. However, focus on His Word and will, rather than on the tool.

For example, for us to do what we do as a church, we have to prosper. We have all kinds of outreach programs, events and services we offer, and I'm full of ideas for more. Every time I get a good idea, somebody on staff yells, "How much will it cost?" Usually my ideas cost a lot! But, if it's His idea, I take it to Him. *God you really want to do this?* Money is the tool to accomplish what we really want to do, such as saving marriages, helping children to know God's will and purpose for their life, bringing in the lost, and developing people into devoted followers of Christ.

I spent three years observing as I was seeking Him for His calling for me. I was seeking and observing. It's all about observing His teachings and commandments. Observe, observe, observe, then you *do*. We're not talking about the *do* yet. This is "O." This is Observe. This is the part about paying attention, noticing, watching, and investigating.

BIBLICAL OBSERVERS

The Bible is full of the *observe* process. When David arrived back at Ziklag, the city was burned down and the families of all his men were carried off. He was discouraged. Everybody spoke of stoning him. He soaked in God. He encouraged himself in the Lord, he soaked in God and he got direction. *What should I do?* He observed God's leadership and found out exactly what to do.

In another example, an angel shows up and starts talking to Gideon: "You're a mighty man." Gideon says, "What are you talking about?" He has to go through a process. Because Gideon has a question, he has to take a journey of seeking God and observing His answer. He was investigating with his fleece.

Consider this: how many times did you have to hear that God loved you before you believed it and said yes to Him? How many times did you have to be invited before you said yes? How long did it take you to become a generous giver in the kingdom of God? How long did it take you to start serving in God's house? It most likely wasn't the first time you heard it.

You had to start processing and observing. *I'm going to observe what God is trying to say...God is that you? I'm trying to figure this out. I'm trying to make sense out of this. I'm trying to understand.* You're not going to live by faith until you first observe.

In fact, people who try to live by faith without first observing, I wouldn't call it faith. I would call it foolishness, because foolishness doesn't count the risk. I do a lot of things by faith, but I know what it could cost me by doing it.

When you know the cost, it isn't foolish. I'm willing to pay the price to lean forward. Does that make sense? If something doesn't work out, I'll never be mad at God, because, in my mind, if it doesn't work out it's a price I'm willing to pay. Therefore, because I observed, I wasn't rash or foolish.

WATCH AND LISTEN

A lot of people don't know how to observe. They don't know how to lean forward a little bit further in God. It's easy to start praying – that's the seeking God part. It's the listening that gets really scary.

For me, it's about listening as I go. *What did You just ask me, God? What did You just suggest that I do with my life? What are you suggesting that I do with my time and my money?*

Remember Gideon, he didn't get that part yet. He had to process in a different way. He had to throw out a bunch of fleeces and get a sign from God. Moses observed something unusual – a bush on fire that wasn't being consumed. He probably thought *that's bizarre over there. I need to investigate that bizarre sight.*

He is talking to himself. He is talking to the sheep. "Hey, sheep, do you... uh, I wish you could talk. Do you see that?" Notice the bush does not start talking until he gives it his attention. God's leadership, God's miraculous manifestation and God's revelation does not start coming into our life until we start observing; until we start paying attention.

Maybe you can relate to this: you went to church. You heard the gospel message, and it suddenly captured your attention. Maybe we read something in God's Word, and we started investigating. We started to seek Him a little bit. All of a sudden, He started drawing us in. He starts prompting us towards something. This is like a live chat with that still, small voice. Are you catching this?

IGNORE DISTRACTIONS

In 1 Kings 19, Elijah traveled over 200 miles to get into God's presence, because he was very confused. Have you ever been very confused? Maybe you're in the midst of a confusing year, or you have a tough decision to make. Have you ever done something that didn't quite work out the way you thought it was going to? I think we all have. That's what happened to Elijah.

Elijah has to go back and recalibrate something. He journeyed 200 miles to seek God. Elijah is desperate to hear His voice. He gets on a mountain, and then into a cave. The Bible says when he was there, the Lord spoke to him, 'Go out, and stand on the mountain before the Lord.' And behold, the Lord passed by, and a great and strong wind tore into the mountains and broke the rocks in pieces before the Lord." That is a serious wind when rocks are blowing over the place, cracking on one another! "... but the Lord was not in the wind; and after the wind an earthquake, but the Lord was not in the earthquake; and after the earthquake a fire, but the Lord was not in the fire; and after the fire a still small voice." Elijah recognized that voice. "So it was, when Elijah heard it, that he wrapped his face in his mantle and went out and stood in the entrance of the cave. Suddenly a voice came to him, and said, 'What are you doing here, Elijah?'"

What are you doing here? This is the observation phase. We're trying to process *what's God asking of me? What's God trying to say to me?* We're trying to figure this out.

Notice He wasn't in the wind. He wasn't in the earthquake, nor in the fire. See, people easily get caught up in all kinds of noisy, flashy movements. They get caught up in somebody else's excitement. They get caught up in somebody else's agenda. They get caught up in somebody else's argument. In the political world, this goes on all the time. We get divisive and caught up in the latest issue and fight.

Can I tell you something? Laws don't change hearts, the Spirit of God does. Let me ask you this question: do you think some Christians spend more time complaining about political issues than they spend praying about them? It's easy to get caught up in the earthquake, get caught up in the fire, and get caught up in the wind. Instead, learn how to get into that still place where you hear the gentle, delicate whisper of the Spirit of God. At the end of the day, God's not going to ask you what your political party did.

In fact, God's not even going to ask you what your church did, either. God's going to ask you what *you* did. Often, some of the people complaining the most about the church are those who do the least in it. I'm not trying to beat anybody up. I'm just trying to explain that if you don't know how to soak in God's presence, you will sour, because when we soak, we soften, we absorb, and we come under His influence. When we soak, we release our giftedness.

If you're not releasing your giftedness, you're not soaking. If you're not really living with the spirit of faith, adventure and hope, you're not living under His influence. If you're not staying soft, then you need a personal revival.

OBSERVE AND OBEY

As I mentioned, for three years I was in a "Gideon phase" of observing. *God, You've got to reveal this to me. I'm not going to go half-cocked. I'm not going to jump into this half-hearted. I have to know that I know that I know...no doubts, no looking back. When I cross this bridge, I'm not coming back, so I must be confident. I must know You've gone before me and have prepared the way.*

God, please pardon me if I'm slow, but I just want to take the time to observe what You're calling me to do. I needed to get past the earthquake and past the fire. I needed to get past the wind. I needed to hear His voice for myself, so that I could observe to know what I was about to do with my life.

Now, 25 years later, I have no regrets. After all this time, I don't wish I would have done something else with my life. I observed His promptings and obeyed.

TRUST

I'm telling you if you will *SOAK* and observe, He will direct your path and you will have good success and you will prosper in the thing that He has called you to do. I can't talk about your story, because I'm not living your life. You will have your own amazing journey with God. God is encouraging you to do something. If you'll start seeking, you'll start to recognize He is encouraging you to do something.

I want to give you a couple more illustrations about what it means to observe. We've already discussed Joshua when he told the people to "consecrate yourself, for tomorrow the Lord will do amazing things among you." Remember, consecration comes before amazing.

Separating yourself to seek God for His purposes always comes before the miracles of God, the manifestations of God, the awesomeness of God, and the awe of God. Consecration always ends in awe. I hope I can deposit that truth in your spirit. If you consecrate yourself, there will always be spiritual growth perks in your life ending in awe.

Now, what if we do that corporately, as the body of Christ? What if we as a church body go into a season of consecrating ourselves? Let's drop our bitterness. Let's let go of resentments. Let's start really walking in what it means to love one another. Let's really say, "God, we're dependent upon Your leadership and trusting in You. We're going to fall in love with You. We're going to serve You, and we're going to serve Your family. I want to share Your love with my city." There is personal consecration, but there's also corporate consecration.

Let's pick up on the rest of Joshua's story. After telling the people to consecrate themselves, Joshua says this, "Tell the priests who carry the Ark of the Covenant: 'When you reach the edge of the Jordan's waters, go and stand in the river.'" A couple verses later we learn that the Jordan is at flood stage all during harvest. Yet as soon as the priests who carried the ark reached the Jordan and their feet touched the water's edge, the water from upstream stopped flowing. They got their feet wet, and then God stopped the flowing river so they could cross.

Next, "The priests who carried the Ark of the Covenant of the Lord stopped in the middle of the Jordan and stood on dry ground, while all Israel passed by until the whole nation had completed the crossing on dry ground." Priests (that's you), catch the backdrop of this story. They are within eyesight of a 400-year-old promise. They're within a short distance of taking hold of a promise that God gave to Abraham, Isaac and Jacob.

They are on the verge of the supernatural. Behind them, not just physically but literally behind them, was a generation that would not trust God. If they're unwilling to get their feet wet, they, too, might be another generation who dies within arms distance of the promise. Sometimes, because we will not follow God's crazy promptings and won't get our feet wet, we don't see what He does.

PRIESTS

You have to understand that you and I, if we're believers, we're priests in our generation. You're a priest in your generation, and you have a congregation. You may not want a congregation, but you have one. If you have an office, you've got a congregation. If you have a co-worker, they're your congregation. The people around you are the ones you need to pray for and teach, love and coach, and bring life to.

You're a priest. Priests stood in the middle of the river, and it was still flowing as they stepped in. Somebody was willing to observe a crazy instruction from God, the crazy prompting from the Lord, and go first.

As long as the priests stood there, the river stopped and backed up. As they were standing there in the middle of the river, people crossed over on their faith. See it deeper: people are crossing over *on* them. For example, some of you are living in the inheritance that you didn't create, on the foundation that you didn't lay. Someone else went ahead of you and stood in faith for something. Now, you are able to cross over into something they fought for. Because they stood in a flooding river, you're now inheriting something heavenly.

I could mention ministry after ministry with leaders who stand in faith and others cross over on their faith; crossing over from the edge of the promise into the promise. We hear stories all the time of people crossing over into God's promises. We hear stories of people being rescued by God because they stood on His promises. Understand that when you give offerings and tithes you're supplying resources to the ministry, and people are crossing over on your faith. It's your turn to be an example in faith and follow some crazy promptings of God.

I pray that you can see this! People are crossing over when you and I live by faith. Here is what a lot of people do though. They look at the Jordan, and they say, "It's not the right time. Let's wait till it's summer and it's dried up, small and easier. Now's not the time." Other times, people say, "We're waiting on God to stop the river. We're waiting on God to dry up the river." While they're waiting on God, God is waiting on them, because they don't know how to recognize His crazy promptings.

Matthew 18 tells us that "whatever you bind on earth will be bound in heaven, and whatever you loose on earth will be loosed in heaven." Think about this: during prayer, we "bind." Literally, that means we come into a contract with something. To *bind* refers to a contract. You buy a car, and you have a binding contract. You buy a house, and you are tied to a binding contract. God is saying He wants to create binding contracts with us in prayer long before we ever see the physical contract.

In other words, when you soak in God's presence, you start getting that settled on the inside of you... all of a sudden you soaked in that first contract, if you will. You bound yourself to this new thing. You're saying it doesn't matter if the river is high or low. Either way it's going to take a miracle for us to cross the river, so if this is the time to go, then let's go.

"But those who wait on the Lord shall renew their strength. They shall mount up with wings like eagles; they shall run and not be weary, they shall walk and not be faint." –Isaiah 40:31

IT'S YOU

When you and I begin to *SOAK* in God's presence, it starts changing who we are. It causes us to absorb and come under the influence of what He wants us to be, and we start releasing out of our lives what we were created for. And, before you see the revival around you that you may be longing for, it starts with you.

Consider this. As a pastor of a church, before revival comes, before we are a vitalized church as a whole, it starts with me. I have got to have a personal, vitalized relationship with God. But, I also know that if you, also, have a relationship with God and you have a personal renewal inside of you, there will be revival within *us*. And, if there is a renewal and a revival within us, then all of a sudden, you will be influencers wherever you go. Because, remember, every person who is a follower of Christ has a congregation. You have a flock. You have people to shepherd. You have people to love. You have people to teach. You have people to visit. You have people who need the Jesus in you.

The church is not a building. *You* are the church. You are the salt of the world, and it does not take a lot of salt to change the flavor of something. Hello somebody!

Do you realize a believer in an office can change the flavor of the office? How about a believer in a family changing the flavor in a family? A believer on a team or a believer in a classroom...or the believer in a neighborhood can change the flavor of it if that believer is experiencing a renewal and passion on the inside of them.

It's true. When you start seeking Him, He will start giving you some of His ideas, and you are going to sit there and say, "What?!" He will stretch you. He is going to challenge you. He wants to expand *you*. And, that is the "O": observe.

A = Act in Faith

Now it's time for the letter "A": *Act* in faith. This is where you start stepping out in faith. This is where your preparation takes action.

VITALIZED, TODAY

If you don't start moving in faith, you will start living in yesterday's memories. If you are not living out of a burning desire, you are living out of yesterday's memories. If you are not living out of your dreams and visions...if you are not living out of hope inspired by the Spirit of God, you are living out of your memories of past places, past experiences and past breakthroughs in God.

Mature believers, mature saints, don't live in yesterday. We need you vitalized *today*. God's not done with you. We need a generation going before us and showing us the way. Stay excited. Stay vitalized. How do you do that? You stay fresh in God, and you keep letting Him ask you to do things by faith. Keep allowing Him to teach you.

When you start stepping out in faith, this is where the real adventure begins! The real journey of discovery begins at the first step: the journey of faith. It's a process to learn to walk by faith. Too many people live their Christianity out of their intellect and logic or out of their Bible study, but not out of their engagement with the Spirit of God on a journey of faith.

When you engage and act, you'll get some adrenaline flowing through your veins. When you engage, your heart gets pounding again. You'll feel alive on the inside. Desperation cries out, "God, you'd better come through! I need you. God, I am trusting You. Where are You, God?

I am dependent on You. I am desperate for You, God." This is actually a good place to be. **Never get to the place in your spiritual walk where you're so comfortable by the blessing of God, that you no longer need Him.**

God, You got me the job, You got me the family, You got me some money, I got my retirement plan, I got my health, I got my mind, I'm clean, I'm sober, I'm together. Thank You. I feel good. I feel safe. You've blessed me. I'm grateful, but I don't need You anymore...unless I go back into crisis, then I'll need you again.

SHAPED BY FAITH

There's a type of *crazy* where people whip up crisis intentionally. Seriously, you've seen it. But, even people who live prudently experience bad things in this life; things which are no fault of their own.

Everyone's lives can be quickly shaped by defining moments; negative defining moments. *I was betrayed. I was abused. I was lied to. I was cheated on. I was abandoned. I was victimized. I got cancer.* Bad things happen. But even so, there's a bold group of people who still seek Him and observe. *What are you asking me to do?*

Despite the circumstances, they find the courage to act, and all of a sudden, they have stories to tell you about getting out of the boat and walking on water; crazy-good stories. They have stories about talking to burning bushes. They have stories to tell you about miracles, because now they aren't being shaped by the negatives, they are being shaped by faith.

I am not saying that once you start a faith journey, you won't have negatives anymore. What I am saying is that life has negatives, but that doesn't have to be your entire story! Your story can be about stepping out in faith, trusting God. Please catch this: **the promises of God must be pursued to be inherited, and they're yours to inherit.**

DAY AND NIGHT

There was a generation who traveled to the Jordan River, and the promise was on the other side. They would not pursue it, so they did not inherit it. This reminds us that we are not going to see God move on our behalf until we get our feet wet.

Everybody else may look around and say, "The river is too big. If God wants me to cross the river, He will dry it up for me." They are waiting on God to do it, and He is waiting on them to take a step in. Defining your life by faith means you're going to have to take some action. And, in taking the action, sometimes it feels crazy...it's a wild ride. That's why so few people make the journey to the point of action.

Let's go back to the thought of meditating day and night. How often does Joshua 1:8 say we should meditate on God's Word? Day and night. Day and night. Some of you spend huge amounts of time meditating on your favorite NFL team. Mine is the Seattle Seahawks, although as I mentioned, it's no longer what I meditate on! But, many meditate on their favorite sports team day and night. You know what I'm talking about.

You're starting to look like a fan. You have seen highlights over and over and over. You're looking for every piece of information that comes out: any quote, comment, tweet, etc. You've read the analysts' predictions on who is going to win. You know the weather forecast. You've got it all down. You're even wearing the gear. Your face is painted with the team colors. You are definitely meditating, a lot... day and night.

If you're a Seahawks fan, you might have some friends who don't get you. They don't understand you, because they're a 49ers fan! They don't believe in what you believe. They don't see what you see. They don't get what you get. Really though, they're just like you, but they meditate on something else.

Just like you start taking on an identity, a perception and a world view from what you meditate on, if you will meditate in God's presence, if you will meditate on God's words, it will influence you. You will start coming under the influence of the Holy Spirit. And, just like people can tell when you've been with Sports Center and NFL Network or even the home shopping channel, the gym, the stock market, or whatever else has your focus, they will also know when you have been with Jesus. It won't be because of the cross you wear around your neck or the fish bumper sticker on your car. There will be something in your personhood, in your face, that will be evident. They'll know *this person has been with Jesus.*

I cannot tell you to go live by faith if you are not intoxicated on the Spirit. If you aren't taking Him in, if you are not internalizing, if you are not absorbing, if you are not drinking up the Spirit, if you are not soaking it up...if you are not coming under the influence, you won't step out in faith.

Really count the costs before you engage in a direction

with your life. That's the, "Okay, God. What are you really saying to me? What is the price I'll need to pay to follow You, and am I willing to pay it?" conversation. We seek, we observe, and then we *do*.

I have to *do*. God is not going to do it for me. God is going to teach me and enable me, and I must choose to engage. He is going to inspire me that I may do according to all that is written. All of us have prayed, "God you do it!" God responds, "No. I will teach you to do it. I will show you the way. I will provide for you. I will bless you. I will go before you and make room for you. Count on Me to do all these things as you take the action step of faith."

Think about it like this: Mom and Dad provide the house, but the child doesn't mature if Mom and Dad keep cleaning their room for them. *It's your room, you clean it.* God is saying, "I am going to provide you the context of your life. But, you have got to provide the *do* within the context of your life. Observe to do, according to all that is written, and then you will make your way prosperous."

DIRECTION

Sooner or later, I have to get my feet wet. I have to get out of the boat and engage with what He has shown me. So, what is He encouraging you to do, and when will you do it?

Proverbs 16:9 says, "A man's heart plans his way, but the Lord directs his steps." Notice, a man's heart plans his way. Sometimes we don't get direction from God because we don't have a plan. God says "You show me a plan. I will give you some direction." People say, "God, what do you want me to do?" which is a valid question. At some point, God says, "Show me a plan. I will give you some direction." I believe this principle.

I seek God regularly. I meditate on God's Word. I know my calling. Recently, I had a plan and submitted it to God. I felt like God said, "That's not going to do. That is just not going to do." *Well, now what?* And, boom...so powerfully, He said, "I want you to think about the next 25 years of your life. I want you to think about the next 25 years of Capital Christian Center. Global, national, regional, local." *Wow, God, I'm clear.* With that message from Him, I'm clear.

The *how* of it is still vague...I have no idea what it "looks" like, but I just know to say *yes*. Clarity. Yes. Confusion. Yes. Do I need God? Yes. Can I figure this out without God? No. Will it take God? Yes. Act in faith, and that means sometimes you won't have complete under-standing of your situation and circumstances. What makes sense to us really doesn't matter, because then we try to lean on our own understanding.

I'm stepping into the river. My foot is out of the boat. God, for this to happen, You have to show up, and that's where the real journey begins. Seek Him, and He will reveal Himself. Seek Him, say yes, and see His power. Seek Him, and see Him come through.

After this revelation, I called up one of my friends and discussed the "global" thought God started brewing in me. My friend began to tell me this story.

One Sunday, my pastor spoke about taking the gospel of Christ into every nation in the world. There are 197 nations, and he wanted to send people from his church to all 197 nations. He gave that message on a Sunday morning. There was a gentleman in our congregation who turned to his wife and said, "Who do you think in this church would be able to do that?" She looked back and replied, "I don't know. But, I know you could."

This man was a corporate executive who turned corporations around. He went into his office that week and decided he wanted to volunteer and help with this effort. Through the pastor's message, his wife's encouragement and the Spirit of God's prompting, this man spent the next 16 months volunteering with that effort and learned a lot about leadership logistics. In the last 10 years, that church has sent over 23,000 people out of its church to all 197 nations on the planet.

What am I saying? We don't know the amazing things God has planned. After that conversation and hearing that story, I still didn't know exactly what my part of

God's global plan was. We don't know. But, hearing that story increased my faith. Someone else heard a global call, too, and took action.

A CONVICTION

When you're sensing what God is leading you to do, no matter what signs come, no matter what wonders come, no matter what doors open, no matter what favor comes, no matter what people you meet, you must internalize the call. And, it must turn into a conviction, not just a feeling.

If you jump into action with a *feeling*, you will drown. Jump out only with faith and a conviction. However, it may take time for that sense and prompting to grow into a conviction. Allow it that time, which is the observation phase (with investigation).

Trust me, people don't know how to do this very well. Having a feeling for the moment is easier. This is why people live together unmarried, because they don't know how to make a commitment. *What if it doesn't work out? What if we don't make it?* But, here's good news: once you make the decision, once it becomes a conviction, even if it doesn't work out you will never be a victim. Once I conclude, *this is what I sense God wants me to do with my life*, no matter how it turns out, I am okay with whatever price it may cost me.

But, if you jump in just feeling something, then if God doesn't show up the way you think He's supposed to, or it doesn't work out according to your plan, you will be offended at Him. He is asking us to follow Him with conviction – faith, not a feeling. At times, faith can be rooted in emotion, and it may start in emotions. But, it has got to move to the intentionality of our will born in our conviction. That's where **emotions and our will merge together to create a commitment in us**.

I see people go off half-baked all the time. Sure, get clarity and do the crazy stuff God asks you to, but be prepared to live with the consequences and never blame God, never blame a pastor, never somebody else. It's your decision. You chose to get out of the boat. You chose to get into the river. You chose to walk by faith. No matter what turns out, be okay with the decision. Be under His influence as you go.

CRAZY COURAGE

Okay, God. I am sensing You. I am feeling You. I am under Your influence. I am losing my mind. It would be good for some of you to lose your mind and get His.

Did you catch that? Some of us need to go crazy and lose our minds so we can get His. Some of your friends will say, "You are going to quit partying and start going to church? You are crazy..." Yeah, I know. I am going to get crazy!

Be honest. How many times has God led you down paths and you said, "This is crazy!" And, the crazier you got, the more of His mind you gained. Why? Because you got rid of your worldly, crazy mind to get His sound mind.

God told Joshua, "Have I not commanded you? Be strong and courageous. Do not be afraid; do not be discouraged, for the Lord your God will be with you wherever you go" (Joshua 1:9). **God may appreciate your attempts at courage more than your attempts at holiness.**

God just might be looking for courage more than He's looking for holiness. *What do you mean by that, Pastor?* Don't misunderstand it. I see so many people in the church world endeavoring to be holy, but unfortunately I think there's another word for it: it's called *fear. Don't be around anything bad. I don't want to be around bad people. I don't want bad things.* Fear is at the root of their actions.

Desire to be holy in your life, attitudes and actions, certainly. But, it takes a lot of courage to say, "God, I surrender." It takes courage to look in the mirror and say, "I need a change." It takes courage to say, "God, I am going trust You." Those declarations might not feel holy, but trust me, God's going to be pleased. *Your holiness does not qualify you. You will never be holy enough.*

In fact, the only thing that will disqualify you is a lack of faith. *God, I trust you. You've got to do it. You have to help change me. I can't do it myself, God.* That's the whole idea of Scripture. When the leper reached out, he was unclean, but Jesus touched him. Do you understand? It was unlawful for the priest to touch lepers. But, Jesus, the Priest, said, "I am going to break the law right here, because after I touch you, you won't be unclean anymore."

The woman who ran into the room with the flask of expensive oil to pour on His feet and head...guess where she got that oil? With the money she made as a prostitute. That pouring of oil was the releasing of her past guilt and signifying her future hope. She said *I am going to worship with what was my profession and now will become my profession of faith.* Are you catching this?

What will you do? It's going to take courage.

BURNED AWAY

Do you know what God wants out of you more than any other thing? That you would be conformed to the image of Christ. It is going to take courage to grow into the image of Christ. For some of us, it means we may need to burn some bridges.

In 1 Kings 19, there's a story of two prophets: Elijah and Elisha. After God spoke to Elijah on the mountain (where he went because he was discouraged), he comes down from the mountain and comes up to someone (who is not a prophet) named is Elisha. "So Elijah went from there and found Elisha son of Shaphat. He was plowing with twelve yoke of oxen." Twelve yoke means there was two pairs of twelve, totaling 24 oxen. This is a big field! "...and he himself was driving the twelfth pair." It is believed that this was at Elisha's family farm. At that time, to have an ox was a big deal. To have two of them was a really big deal. To have 24 of them was a massive deal.

"Elijah went up to him and threw his cloak around him. Elisha then left his oxen and ran after Elijah. 'Let me kiss my father and mother goodbye,' he said, 'and then I will come with you.' 'Go back,' Elijah replied. 'What have I done to you?'" Pause right there for a moment.

Elisha is working, plowing his family's field. There is something big going on the inside of him. Something big: God. There's something else: success. *I have success. I've got prosperity. I am set, God. I have my family's property.*

I am set, God. But, this isn't it. That's not all...there's more.

There's more! When Elijah throws his cloak on him, he is calling Elisha to ministry. He is calling him to follow God. Elisha runs up to him and says, "Okay, I'm in! Just let me go say goodbye to my mom and dad." Elijah acts nonchalant about it. *I don't care. I am not talking you into anything. Whatever.*

Watch what it goes on to say: "So Elisha left him and went back. He took his yolk of oxen and slaughtered them. He burned the plowing equipment to cook the meat and gave it to the people, and they ate. Then he set out to follow Elijah and became his servant."

Do you know what he was doing? He was burning a bridge. *Goodbye old life. I am never coming back. This God thing is too attractive. It is too inviting. Mom, Dad, please don't be mad at me, but I have got to go. Guys, I got to go. I am going to burn this equipment. I can't be tempted to come back to it. I am going to burn my inheritance. I am not coming back to it. I am getting it out of my system.*

Literally, after he ate the food and it was digested, he got it out of his system. Gross, yes, but a good metaphor. God is trying to take us on a journey, and we have to get our past out of our system. Past failure must get out of your system. Even past successes have to get out of your system, too. Get your past disappointments out of your system. The ways of your past have to get out. The history of who you used to be has to get out. Then, say hello a new life.

LETTING GO TO TAKE HOLD

Most people live plan B because plan A is too scary. Most people live a plan B life because plan A is too intimidating. Plan A means *I am going to trust God completely.* Plan A means *I am going to have to really rely on God.* Plan A means *I am going to have to sweat this thing out with God.* Plan A means *I am going to live with a sense of desperation in my life,* and since that's too scary, we live in safe, small, plan B. **Plan B is what's comfortable, what's easy, what's normal, what's okay.**

Again, I'm like Elijah who says, "If you want to go back, that's okay. I don't care. That is between you and God." I am not trying to beat anybody up or seem callous. But, I am telling you that once you start coming under the influence, you are going to start having some crazy dreams and new desires. You'll start getting influenced, and He will start encouraging you to do something. If you decide not to step across that line of faith and get your feet wet, then your dreams will wither, leaving you with a meager life of living off yesterday's memories.

Remember the woman with the valuable alabaster flask of oil? The oil in it was worth a year's wage. The jar she carried it in was most likely a family heirloom. She broke it like it was a cheap clay pot and poured out all its contents on Jesus. She made a mess. The smell of it perfumed the whole house. Everybody freaked out. Judas was all freaked out. *What are you doing? Why waste all that money?*

She's making a scene. *I am not going back. I am not going back. I am all in. I am laying my life down. I am going forward.*

Don't rush that kind of decision. I am not saying all decisions made quickly are purely emotional, but take time to wrestle it out, pray it out, process it out, and think it out. When it's something God is obviously directing you to do, get so miserable you can't stay the same unless you jump in.

THE CHOICE IS YOURS

I remember when I was working for the city before Capital Christian Center was established. I was seeking God, but I was also pursuing career development. Finally, I had received a promotion to the position I'd been pursuing! It was the position I wanted, and I had favor. It was mine! And then, God said, "Now is the time." Was this a test?

In that time, I had a dream. He can give dreams to those who are under the influence of seeking God. I was under the influence, on my journey. In this dream, I am preaching to a small audience, maybe ten people, in a little, old church with benches and pews (you know... those hard pews), and no one is interested in what I am saying. I remember sweating. It was very hot. I'm shouting passionately, preaching my heart out, but stone faces are looking back at me. Was I wasting my time? Hardly any people, no interest. I'm laboring to get my point across, and I invite people to give their life to Christ.

One little boy came to the front for the altar call. He was probably eight years old. I remember bowing down and looking down at him, and he's saying, "I want Jesus in my life." And then, in the moment, the dream shifted.

Before me was a white house with a white picket fence and manicured yard: the American dream. I felt the Spirit of God say, "The choice is yours. You can have your career or you can have Mine." Honestly, he didn't make His choice look attractive at all. I said, "God it is not a choice. I have got to follow You. I have got to. I am just crazy, God, but knowing that I reached that one life was all the reward I needed."

That was nearly 30 years ago. It took me a couple of years to get here, but I have never regretted it or looked back.

BACK TO THE BASICS

Where will you start taking action? Don't make it weird. **You don't need deeper interpretation, you need clearer application.** When scripture says forgive one another, you don't need to have a word study on what *forgive* another person means. You just need to search your heart and ask *who do I need to forgive?* After that, ask yourself if you'll actually do it, and when? You probably don't even need a lot of time to process through that. You don't need more clarification, just application.

When the Bible says in Matthew 22 to love your neighbor as yourself, we don't need to act like Pharisees who question Jesus about who our neighbor is. It's easy to figure out who our neighbors are. Just ask, "God, who do I start with? Who are the five people I need to love this week? Who is the person I need to call this week?" It's like when Scripture says do everything without grumbling or arguing. Does that really need more explanation? No, it's self-explanatory.

Here's some great advice about taking action on what God says: start taking action on basic godly principles that apply to everyone before you try and jump into what is specific to you. Are you born again? Have you been water baptized? Are you planted in His house? Are you serving? Are you doing the things that are basic Christianity?

Here's the funny thing. People who get caught up in emotional decisions and decide *I am going to do something* by *"faith,"* but aren't doing what is basic in the Bible, those are the people who sabotage their lives. But, it shows wisdom to start with the basics, and then clarity will come for what God has to say specifically to you.

K = KEEP YOUR FAITH ALIVE

The phrase *keep the faith* is used a lot. But, it's not just keep the faith... .it's *keep your faith alive.* We've reached our last letter in our *SOAK* acronym, "K," and that's what it stands for: *Keep* your faith alive.

Believe, Then Do

Alive! Faith should be vibrant, full of energy, in movement, and going forward, not just still and sedentary, hoping that something happens. No, full of vibrancy, alive.

James 2 verse 22 says something interesting (Message translation): "Wasn't our ancestor Abraham 'made right with God by works' when he placed his son Isaac on the sacrificial altar? Isn't it obvious that faith and works are yoked partners, that faith expresses itself in works? That the works are 'works of faith'?" Yes! Our faith expresses itself in works.

It goes on to say, "The full meaning of 'believe' in the Scripture sentence, 'Abraham believed God and was set right with God,' includes his action. It's that mesh of believing and acting that got Abraham named 'God's friend.' It is evident that a person is made right with God not by a barren faith but by a faith fruitful in works. The same with Rahab, the Jericho harlot.

In the case of Rahab, the Bible is talking about a woman who was made right by God, not about all the sins she had committed. This translation literally calls her a 'Jericho harlot.' That's pretty low. All too often we think we need to get right with God by doing all of these perfect things and knowing all the right biblical answers. But, the Bible's so clear that isn't the requirement.

What was it about Rahab? Was it her action in hiding

God's spies and helping them escape? It was her seamless unity of believing and doing. What counted with God? She had heard of Israel's powerful God, believed in His power and acted according to His will. She listened to His voice and immediately put that into action.

It doesn't matter where you're at in life today, how dirty and slimy you may feel in your situations, in your faults, and in your failures. God will still speak to you, just like He did with Rahab. Your part is acting on what He's asked and called you to do. It's that beautiful mesh of believing, and then doing.

BELIEVING

As Christians, we're incredible believers. We call ourselves believers, right? But, let's be sure we understand the biblical definition of believing. It's not a sedentary, sit down and agree on something believing, it's a get-out-of-my-chair, put it into action, and do it in my life believing.

The Bible says in the book of James: "Don't just be hearers of the word, but be doers also." If you're believing in something from God in your life, it is so much more than just sitting down and praying about it. Pray, then get out of the prayer closet and put something into action to see it come alive.

At the end of James chapter 2 it says, "The very moment you separate body and spirit, you end up with a corpse. Separate faith and works and you get the same thing: a corpse." No longer can we deceive ourselves and think *if I just pray hard enough, then that's what faith really is. If I just get enough wishful thinking and optimistic attitude about my situation and send enough good thoughts towards it...then God will come in and do something.* No. It's this beautiful meshing completely together.

Faith cannot be separated from works. God is calling you to lead a life of faith. The Bible says in Hebrews, "Without faith it's impossible to please God." If God is calling you to live a life of faith, it is absolutely tied to getting into action about what God has called you to do.

ROUTINE

Nobody can do for you what God has called you to do. Nobody else can put into action, the dreams, the plans, and the promises He's made you, the things that you are believing God for other than you. So, what's stopping you? What's holding you back from rushing straight into the beautiful, amazing, incredible promises that God has called you to? Is it fear? Is it worry? Are you over-whelmed?

"Some lose their footing in the faith completely" (1 Timothy 6:10). Remember, the belief system itself won't do it: it's belief and action. The rest of that verse says, "and live to regret it bitterly ever after." See, as believers, I know a lot of us who still absolutely believe in Jesus Christ, but have long since stopped putting that belief into action. They've allowed the circumstances of their lives to pull them down to places of depression, isolation and frustration against God.

This arms-length familiarity with godly things breeds contempt. I think familiarity also breeds numbness. All too often we come to church and make it a routine. It should be sacred, full of wonderful purpose, rejuvenating us through worship, growing in God, using our gifts and abilities to serve other people, and sharing God's love with those far from Him. It truly is a beautiful thing God designed, and we seem to recognize that at first. But, after a few years go by, it erodes, and our belief and action can turn into a sedentary belief.

We come into service, sit down, stand up, read the song lyrics, clap at the message, get up, say hello to some friends, go home, and return back to a normal life. According to 1 Timothy 6, some lose their footing in the faith completely, the freshness fades in their hearts, and they live to regret it bitterly ever after. The Bible doesn't, however, say those that live by faith, who jumped out and did something scary for God, live to regret it. It's those who get too comfortable or become weary, those who turn their faith into a routine who live to regret it.

I understand this is a challenging message, but my purpose for sharing it is to stir you up. I hope it's enough to spur you on to keep your faith alive. God has given you a purpose and a plan. Not a day goes by that God doesn't want you to do something amazing and incredible for His kingdom. Did you know there are only two things we can do here on earth that we can't do in Heaven? One is sin (there is no sin in Heaven), and the other is going after and loving those far from God (everyone in Heaven is saved). That's it! Of those two things, which do you think God left us here to do after we were born again?

Not a day of our life should go by that we don't live in faith and action, showing God's love to those far from Him. Not a day should go by that we go into work, count the hours and minutes until we get to leave, and remain unaware of the incredible things God wants to do in our life. If you're not sure yet, then go back to the beginning; go back to "S" and seek to know God. *God, what do You want me to do?* You observe His prompting, you act in faith and you keep that faith alive through action.

VIGILANT

Keep your faith alive. Keep your heart! Proverbs 4:23 says, "Keep your heart with all diligence, for out of it spring the issues of life." The Message translation says it like this: "Keep vigilant watch over your heart."

Keep vigilant, diligent watch over your heart: that's where life starts. It's easy to forget about all the common things the enemy tries to use to snare us in the world. I don't know many believers that rush straight into sin, saying, "I'm just going to have one of those days today and mess myself up!" Maybe there are a few, but that's certainly not how it happens to most of us.

What I have found, myself included, is that when we don't keep diligent, vigilant watch over our hearts, it's those little whispers that begin to get us snared. Think about an animal in the forest. It can take a million steps in freedom, but it only takes one in a snare to get it stuck. How true for us, too. We are wise to keep vigilant, diligent watch over what's coming into our hearts.

Here's what I mean. Who says you have to read the news every day and listen to all the fear mongering? You don't have to! God didn't give us a spirit of fear, but of peace, of love, and of a sound mind. So, we watch or read the news and think, *oh I'm just reading the news to be an informed citizen*, except we expose our hearts to fear, just a little bit. We start to live by fear, just a little bit, and now we're snared. Now we aren't living by how God created us, which is supposed to be with courage and boldness, with freedom and peace, because we opened our heart just a little bit.

Who says we have to get caught up in someone else's drama? We check Facebook and get riled up by someone else's drama, and now we're offended by them. We opened the snare just a little bit to that, and now we're upset and caught up, when God has called us to love those far from Him and to be reconcilers; to show people what the forgiveness of Jesus is all about. We watch questionable things on TV. Again, we get our foot caught in the snare so easily.

One of the enemy's number one tactics in making us think sin is normal and to de-sensitize us to it is through entertainment and comedy. Look at the morality today compared to even 10 or 15 years ago. Watch old shows and movies, and notice the pleasure-seeking messages they snuck in or what they were making fun of, and look how it's normal and accepted today.

What are you putting into your heart when you're watching TV? *Oh, it's no big deal. It's just a little comedy. Oh, they're all just living together, sleeping together. That's just normal outside in the world.* Really? What are we putting in our hearts? Are we keeping diligent, vigilant watch over our heart? I'm not talking about becoming some isolated holy club. It's important, because while we are here on earth, we have an incredible purpose and plan from God that we need to be ready to put into action at any minute, at a moment's notice.

In order to keep your faith alive, your heart will need to be guarded from faith-stealing input.

WISE INPUT

Who are you surrounding yourself with? This is another great question to ask yourself as you keep your faith thriving. In 1 Corinthians, the Bible says that bad company corrupts good character. The worst thing you can do, if you're trying to keep your faith alive, is to surround yourself with negative people who tell you that *God's not real*, or *He can't do it*, or *that's not gonna happen*. Unless you are witnessing to those people, don't allow them to have input and a voice into your life.

You control who you have meaningful relationships with, and again, it's not so that we isolate as Christians. We have a very real world we need to bring our love to; God's love. But, we need to be very wise about what we allow into our hearts. Genesis 2:15 says, "The Lord God took the man and put him in the Garden of Eden to tend it and keep it." Before sin entered the world, God placed man to guard and protect this beautiful, wonderful, sacred place.

God also created your heart just like Eden, as this beautiful, wonderful sacred place, and you have a responsibility (just like Adam and Eve did) to tend and keep it. But, what did they do instead? They let one small snare of the enemy cause a whole lot of havoc. Guard your heart. If you've become numb, say, "God, please re-sensitize me. Help me not be so familiar with this stuff. Help it not to be so normal and so customary. God help me to guard my heart."

What kind of music are you listening to? Did you know that psychologists have found that the number one way sexual thoughts enter is not through visual stimulus, but through music? Interesting. Think about what happens on a subconscious level when you listen to perverted music. No wonder why so many struggle with these kinds of thoughts. Guard your heart by guarding your eyes and ears.

RISE ABOVE

In Mark 4, we learn about the Parable of the Sower. In verse 14, Jesus explains that the farmer plants the Word (the seeds represent the Word). Some people are like the seed that falls on the hardened soil of the road. No sooner do they hear the Word than Satan snatches away what has been planted in them. And, some others are like the seed that lands in the gravel, when they first hear the Word they respond with great enthusiasm, but there is such a shallow soil of character that when the emotion wears off and difficulties arrive there is nothing to show for it.

Our faith in action has to rise above our circumstances. All of us can have shallow character at times, but thank God for His endless mercy and grace. All we have to say is, "God, I am sorry. I repent," and He washes it clean. I'm so glad He does not hold our past, forgiven garbage against us. He absolutely doesn't. But, if you want to live a life of faith and action, develop your character. Learn how to press through your circumstances and the difficulty of a situation in order to respond how God has called you to respond.

That's why the Bible teaches us to take captive every rebellious thought and make it obedient to Christ. That is not an easy process, but it's a whole lot easier when we're spending time soaking in His presence, isn't it? It's a whole lot easier when we come into worship and we say, "God, I love You. God, I adore You. You are bigger than my circumstances. You are bigger than my difficulties." We build up pure faith, we respond to what God has called us to do, and this beautiful thing begins to happen in us. When He plants His Word, there's no longer shallow soil, but a rich, meaningful place in our inner man where we can live. But, don't think we're going to respond differently if we don't change some outer man behaviors and patterns. Isn't that the definition of insanity?

Imagine what could happen in your marriage, your finances, or your career if you spent meaningful time soaking in God's presence each day, and then put into motion the things He's asked you to do. Wow, you would feel alive! Even if it's something as simple as showing your employer as much respect as you can, to love your spouse afresh every day, or to treat your children with such tenderness and kindness as if the last week of them screaming at you didn't even happen.

What would happen in your life if you began to put those (simple) things into action?

PLANTINGS

The rest of the teaching in Mark 4 goes on to discuss two more heart soil types: weedy and good. The seeds cast upon the thorns, or weeds, represents the person who hears the good news about Christ and accepts it, but are too overwhelmed with cares and worries about all the things they have to do and all the things they want to get. The stress of their pursuits strangles what they heard and nothing comes of it. The fruit of what the Word should bear gets choked out.

What happens when God comes in and wants to plant a dream in your heart? I'm talking about a big dream, not just a *let's make it through the week* survival goal. What if He planted a dream so big, it took the next 25 years of your life to complete? A vision so expansive that it was just beyond; beyond the routine, beyond the ordinary, an overwhelming dream that God planted in your heart? Would stress, worry, desires for other things, the busyness of life come and strangle that? Or, would you spend time in God's presence and say, "God, help me to water the dream and clear out these weeds. God, don't let the stress of my life or the stress of my circumstances dare threaten the dream You've placed in my heart. God, anytime I begin to listen to fear, stress and overwhelm, help me instantly hear Your voice and get rid of any other voice so I can live in the dream You've called me to."

I'll tell you something right now, Saint, if God has placed a big dream in your heart, don't think it's going to be a cakewalk through the process. The Israelites were in bondage, but to get to the Promised Land there was a journey they all had to take. If you allow God to take you through that journey, the Bible says in the book of James that perseverance will develop maturity, character and faith inside of you and it won't matter what comes your way. You will be able to stand strong… *if* you allow God to work His process in your heart.

It won't be an instant, overnight process, so just be okay with that. Please do not allow stress, worry and the busyness of your today's circumstances threaten the amazing dream God wants to do in your life. You've got this – with His help. The enemy will want to come in and keep you so busy and so worried and so full of stuff to do that God's dream gets pushed out to the side. When that happens, soak and tell the enemy, "No, you are not doing that in my life. I live by peace. I live by strength in God's Word. I trust in my Father, and it doesn't matter what you try to throw at me or how busy you try to make my life. I am in control, and with God's help I can do all things. This dream will come to pass as I soak in His presence and put into action the things He's called me to do."

You've got this. You can do it, but don't let shallow character, stress or worry choke out the dreams and plans God so desperately wants to see come through your life. He has good plans for you.

KEEP A RECORD

In Joshua 4:4, we see something important when it comes to keeping our faith alive. "Then Joshua called the twelve men whom he had appointed from the children of Israel, one man from every tribe; and Joshua said to them: 'Cross over before the ark of the Lord your God into the midst of the Jordan, and each one of you take up a stone on his shoulder, according to the number of the tribes of the children of Israel, that this may be a sign among you when your children ask in time to come, saying, 'What do these stones mean to you?'" One translation says to put the stones up "so you'll have something later to mark the occasion."

In the future, their children will ask, "Dad, what do these stones mean to you? Mom, why are these stones piled up here?" For the children of Israel, these piled up stones served as a memorial forever; forever proclaiming God's deliverance. They'd reply, "The Jordan was stopped in front of the ark of the covenant of God as it crossed the Jordan."

The river stopped in its tracks. These stones were a permanent memorial for the people. If you haven't read this section of the Bible, go read it. It's an incredible story. God, for the second time, was asking the people to do something impossible, coming to a massive river they could not cross: the Jordan River. So, they trusted God, and He literally parted it open once again for them to cross through. And, what Joshua was telling the men who represented each tribe to do was: "I want each of you to go get a stone to place here at the river. When your children come and say, 'Dad, what does that mean?' You can say, 'You know what, Son, when we thought something was impossible, God did the impossible. While you may not have seen it happen, I saw it, and don't you ever forget Who your God is.'" What are the records, the altars and the memorials in your life that remind you of the power and the goodness of God? These memorials are for you *and* the generations to come.

When you come through a struggle and say, "You know, marriage is tough, but with God's help your Mom and I worked it out. Always remember, as you face challenges in your marriage, that *with* God all things are possible. If He can do it in *our* marriage, He can do it in *your* marriage." As you go through things, you can say, "Daughter, I want you to look at this right here. There was a time when Momma got let go from her job, and we didn't know how we were going to pay for the food on the table. But our God is Jehovah Jireh! He provided for all of our needs, and while you go through challenges and you go through difficulties, don't you ever forget who your Jehovah Jireh is. Always know who your provider is and that you can trust Him." Keep a record of His goodness, so when we get busy and we go through tough things in life, we'll never forget the miracles of God.

Remember

When we read about the children of Israel's 40-year journey from slavery into the Promised Land, sometimes we wonder how they could be so stupid after seeing all that God did for them. They repeatedly forgot the plagues that God sent upon Egypt in order to free them and then began to complain to God about their present circumstances. Are we much different?

When we hit rough patches in our life, we tend to think, *God, do you even care about me?* God is probably thinking, *Hello! Do you not see the marriage I restored ten years ago? Do you not remember the time I healed your body? Are you forgetting the time I brought you from captivity into freedom? Don't you ever forget who I Am.*

Our lives should be filled with memorable stories of the goodness of God; stories we never forget. Don't trust your faulty mind to remember everything. Create visual reminders. What are the records and the memorials you're setting up? What will remind you, and generations to come, of who your God is?

It's just like birthdays. I love to celebrate my children's birthdays. Every year we go around the calendar and arrive on these special days, and what do we do? We celebrate God's blessings to us! We celebrate my beautiful daughter and two sons. We now get the privilege of celebrating our grandchildren, too. We honor each other. We cherish each other.

For some of us, there's a sacred place of honor and remembrance when we go to a cemetery. We pay respects and remember someone who meant something to us, and there's a gravestone there to remember them. Holidays are much the same. I used to celebrate Memorial Day by having a bar-b-que, but as the military began to move into our area, I began to understand the great significance behind Memorial Day. Now, I take time to remember and honor those who fought bravely for our country. It's like an altar: it's a memorial to help us remember.

What altars, or memorials, do you have set up in your life to celebrate God? What if you cut out every holiday, every birthday, and you celebrated nothing? Would you remember the specialness or significance of anything? What if there were no graveyards to remember and honor people who have passed?

Here's a tough question: how often, spiritually, do we not celebrate our God or remember the gracious things He's done for us? He deserves the honor and glory! To show Him honor, to have a sacred place of remembrance and to celebrate all He's done is something to get excited about.

I'm telling you what... if you want to live a life of faith and action, one of the easiest ways to do that is to have a life filled with stories of God overcoming. Those instances strengthen you, because every time you face the mountain, you're confident: *I've been here before. God defeated the last 17, he will surely take care of this one.* There is power in trusting God.

WRITE IT

"Write the vision and make it plain" (Habakkuk 2:2) is a verse that encourages us to write down what God speaks to us so that "whoever reads it can run." I encourage you to do that, as well as to write down what you're believing God for. Capital Christian Center does that as a church each January. Each person writes a letter, and at the end of the year we send them back. Those letters act as a memorial to remember what God has done throughout the year. What are you believing God for in this season? Write it down. What did you see Him do last season? Write it down.

"Will the Lord walk off and leave us for good? Will he never smile again? Is his love worn threadbare? Has his salvation promise burned out? Has God forgotten his manners? Has he angrily stalked off and left us?" (The Message, Psalm 77:7-10) Some of us think, "Just my luck... the high God goes out of business just at the moment I need Him." Have you ever felt that way before?

Well, here's the Psalmist's solution: he's going to remember. "Once again I'll go over what God has done, lay out on the table the ancient wonders; I'll ponder all the things you've accomplished, and give a long, loving look at your acts." The longer you live, the more loving, wonderful, miraculous acts you should see, ponder and celebrate. And, don't be selfish. Tell everyone about them! Tell everyone about the goodness of your God.

KEEP YOUR FOCUS

You move in the direction you're focusing on. Matthew 6:22 (The Message) says, "Your eyes are windows into your body. If you open your eyes wide in wonder and belief, your body fills up with light. If you live squinty-eyed in greed and distrust, your body is a dank cellar. If you pull the blinds on your windows, what a dark life you will have!"

You get to choose what to focus your sight on, and if you choose to focus on things like *God is a good God, God loves me, He wants me to win, He's gonna take me from victory to victory, it doesn't matter the challenges I face because God helps me overcome,* then what a wide, wonderful, light-filled life you'll have. But, if you go through life with greed and distrust and when more of your prayers are filled with what you want *from* God rather than what you want *for* God, there's a greed issue in your heart.

Don't get me wrong. The Bible says that we have not because we ask not, and so it's okay to petition Him with our needs. There is a holy, sacred place that God wants us to boldly approach Him, asking for the things we want and desire. But, pay attention to what's coming out of you. Is your prayer life so filled with want, want, want from God out of greed? Do we have prayers filled with distrust, where we throw out a helpful prayer (because we know that's the *Christian* thing to do), but we don't truly believe in our hearts that God will come through?

In James, it says when we pray those kind of prayers, we're like waves of an ocean being tossed to and fro. We are double-minded. When you pray and you're feeling unsettled, go to God and say, "God, I don't know if my emotions feel it right now, but I declare You *are* a good God. I declare You *are* a faithful God. I do not look at my circumstances to tell me who You are. I declare who You are *to* my circumstances. And, I know with You all things are possible. I look forward to Your victory."

Do you see the difference? It doesn't mean you necessarily *feel* that way in the moment, but it's the truth. Use your mouth anyway. The Bible says the tongue is a rudder that steers the ship. Let your words declare it, and your emotions will catch up. Speak those words and pray those words until you've got the *win* on the inside of you. Don't you dare leave that prayer closet until you've got the *win* on the inside of you!

When you come to God, absolutely ask Him for what you want. Absolutely ask Him for what you need, but also stop and ask, "God, what can I do for You? What do You want? How can I bless You, Lord? How can I honor You with my life, Lord? When we begin to do that, we open our focus to this bright, beautiful life filled with God's wonderful goodness.

FOCUS

You've been around those people who complain all day long. They're miserable… and then you feel miserable. On the flip side, you love being around those people who look for the beauty and goodness in everything. That's not a personality. That's a decision. What you keep your focus on is up to you. Make the decision to be a person who looks at the beauty.

What does the Bible teach us in Philippians 4? Whatever is true, noble, just, pure, lovely, is of a good report, virtuous, praise worthy… keep your focus on these things. Meditate on these things. Does that mean bad things won't happen anymore in life? Does that mean negative things don't happen in life? No. In this world we will have troubles, but it means we choose not to focus on troubling things.

I've already decided – I'm choosing to focus on the good, the beautiful, the lovely. Keep your focus. The best example of that is Jesus Christ, who the Bible says, "For the joy set before Him endured the cross." His focus was not the cross, it was not the circumstance, nor the pain. It was the joy! He knew what was coming next. His focus was on all those He would restore to Himself, including you and me. That's what got Jesus through the cross.

What is your focus?

PRIORITIES

You know, even for me as I've been learning and relearning these timeless, biblical truths about soaking in God's presence, I have felt so re-energized, so invigorated, full of passion, and full of renewed vision. No matter what season of life you're in, always make soaking in God's presence a priority.

How do we spend meaningful time in God's presence? How do we grow into spiritual maturity and health and come into what God has for us? How can we know Him? Not just know of Him, but know Him personally? In the book of John, it says that *eternal life is to know God*.

In Greek, the word used for *"to know"* is the same word that was used in Genesis when it said: "Adam *knew* his wife, Eve." There's a very deep, intimate, meaningful relationship that happens as you begin to know God. It is not an intellectual study. It's a oneness, a connection, an interpersonal relationship that God very much desires to have with us. He waits for us to begin that journey of seeking to truly know Him.

Know God, and act in faith on all the things you've observed Him to say as you've soaked. Don't worry about figuring it all out beforehand. As I mentioned, Proverbs teaches us not to lean on our own understanding, but to acknowledge Him in everything, and He'll make our path straight. Simply place your faith in God, and then act on it.

If you haven't already, I encourage you to make the decision to *SOAK* and experience the transforming power of God's presence.

PRAYER

Having a relationship with God starts with repentance. Maybe you don't have a relationship with God yet. The Bible says we must be born again to have a relationship with Him. Maybe you need to reconnect to your relationship with God. Things got going with Him at one point, but life got busy. Something happened, and your relationship with God got disconnected. Pray this out loud:

"Father, today I open my heart and mind to You. I ask You to forgive me of my sins. Help me forgive those who've sinned against me. I ask you to be my Lord and Savior from this day forward. I look to You for leadership in my life. I put my trust in You. In Jesus' Name."

With that prayer comes a new beginning. That's an apology and an acceptance of God into your life. If you prayed that prayer, I encourage you to start reading the Bible. Start talking to God every day. Start coming to church every week. Honor God with your time, and He will meet you there.

STUDY QUESTIONS

Week 1 (pages 7-26):

1. What are two benefits of getting into God's presence? In what way has it personally benefitted you?

2. What's the difference between smart decisions and emotional decisions? Give examples from your life.

3. Why is it important to mature in God?

Week 2 (pages 27-46):

1. What does it mean to you to *SOAK*?

2. What kinds of resistance might you encounter by choosing to *SOAK*? Have you personally encountered resistance?

3. Identify who and/or what might be personal hindrances or might hold you back from taking the *SOAK* journey.

Week 3 (pages 47-67):

1. How does a person create a hunger and a thirst for God? What could you personally do to develop more hunger?

2. What gifts and talents have you discovered through soaking in God's presence?

3. What action can you take today toward living a life of intimacy with God?

Week 4 (pages 68-88):

1. Where in life do you tend to get caught up in distractions?

2. If priests "go first," where do you feel apprehensive in life about going first?

3. Up to this point, would you say your life has been shaped more by your circumstances, or by faith? Explain.

Week 5 (pages 89-106):

1. Do you consider yourself a courageous person? Why or why not? How could you become more courageous?

2. Where in your life do you live with Plan B subconsciously in charge: the easy, safe, comfortable option?

3. Do you feel that your faith is very much alive or has it become routine? Explain.

Week 6 (pages 107-125):

1. What are some ways you could keep a more diligent watch over what's coming in to your heart?

2. What are some of the amazing things God has done in your life? How can you keep a record of them?

3. How can your prayers become less of what you want *from* God and more of what you want *for* God?

For additional copies of *SOAK* for friends, family, Bible study groups, and military service members, please visit
<u>www.go2ccc.org</u> or <u>www.CreativeForcePress.com</u>

Readers, if you've enjoyed this book, would you consider rating it and reviewing it on Amazon.com? Thank you.

About the Author

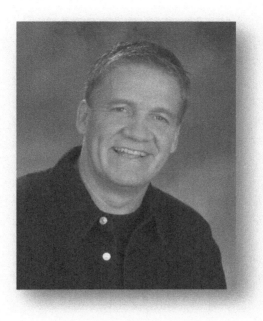

Pastor Dave Minton has been the senior pastor of Capital Christian Center (CCC) in Olympia, Washington, since 1988. Passionate about serving his community, local military personnel and ministry leaders, under the stewardship of Pastor Dave, CCC hosts free community outreach events, military fellowship ministry, celebrate recovery, leadership seminars, Formation school for ministry interns, ministries for children, youth, women and men, and offers more than eight services each week. Pastor Dave is married to Kelly, and together they have five grown children and three grandchildren, with a fourth on the way.

www.go2ccc.org

SOAK is proudly published by:

Creative Force Press

www.CreativeForcePress.com

Do You Have a Book in You?